HOW TO WIN
AT FEMINISM

HOW TO WIN AT FEMINISM

THE DEFINITIVE GUIDE TO HAVING IT ALL—AND THEN SOME!

PRESENTED BY

Reductress

HarperOne
An Imprint of HarperCollinsPublishers

HarperCollins books may be purchased for educational, business, or sales promotional use. For information please e-mail the Special Markets Department at SPsales@harpercollins.com.

HarperCollins website: http://www.harpercollins.com

HarperCollins®, 👑®, and HarperOne™ are trademarks of HarperCollins Publishers.

FIRST EDITION

Designed by Kris Tobiassen / Matchbook Digital

IMAGE CREDITS: *Plinky illustrations*, Carly Monardo, *patron saints*, Steve Dressler, *Rosie the Riveter poster*, J. Howard Miller, *mom #2*, Joanna Nurmis, *mom #3*, Mikhail Koninin, *Madonna*, David Shankbone, *Oprah*, Greg Hernandez, *Whoopi Goldberg*, David Shankbone, *Taylor Swift*, Eva Rinaldi, *Katy Perry*, Eva Rinaldi, *Shailene Woodley*, Georges Biard, *Lassie*, Pleple2000, *patriarchy penis ghost*, Carly Monardo, *woman journaling, woman decorating, woman modeling, woman writing poetry, woman doing crossword, woman holding wine, woman dancing, woman drinking tea, roller derby woman*, iStock, *bad feminist illustrations*, Beth Newell, *coupon*, Tom Pappalardo, *9 layers of Hell illustration*, Tom Pappalardo, *Bruno Mars*, Brothers Le, *Adam Levine*, Karina3094, *Zayn Malik*, Eva Rinaldi, *Lumps ad*, Tom Pappalardo, *Zair ad*, Tom Pappalardo, *ancient Egyptian illustration*, Beth Newell, *Gloria Steinem*, Ms. Foundation for Women, *Gertrude Stein*, Alvin Langdon Coburn, *gracefully aging women*, ©Tabercil, ©Georges Biard, ©Justin Hoch, *fucking-up-kids meter*, Tom Pappalardo, *consoling women*, iStock, *work/life balance chart*, Tom Pappalardo, *43.5 year old mom #1*, ©Jennifer Liseo, *Megyn Kelly*, ©MattGagnon, *Kim Kardashian*, Luke Ford, *women hugging*, Pablo Rogat, *kid painting*, Jim Pennucci, *feminist fortune teller*, Beth Newell, *Ruth Bader Ginsburg*, Steve Petteway, *Vagilante tool*, Beth Newell, *Ellen DeGeneres*, Glen Francis, *meme boats*, Ricardo Eirado, *meme fence*, Dario Sanchez, *marijuana nipples*, iStock, *spirit feminist illustrations*, Beth Newell. All other images courtesy Reductress. All other uncredited original photographs by Kendall Burke.

Library of Congress Cataloging-in-Publication Data is available upon request.

ISBN 978-0-06-243980-2

16 17 18 19 20 RRD(C) 10 9 8 7 6 5 4 3 2 1

CONTENTS

WHAT IS FEMINISM AND WHY AM I THAT NOW?

A lot of people think that feminism just appeared out of nowhere, but it actually took a lot of strong women (and men!)* to get us to the point of complete and total gender equality. But this year, we finally did it! *We won feminism.* And although we have to thank the brave souls who paved the way for us, we mostly want to thank ourselves—Reductress, your favorite women's magazine—for doing it better than everybody else. Now that we, the media, have broken down barriers and made feminism safe for the masses, it's time for you to get on board, girl!

So how did we win feminism? By championing the greatest feminist works of our generation—empowering pop songs, feminist music videos, inspiring advertising, and shows with the word "girls" in the title. Every move we've made—every tearful show recap, every tearful concert viewing, every tearful Instagram scroll—has been decidedly pro-women!

Don't believe that we won? The evidence is clear. You can see it in every living, breathing woman around you. You can see it in her shining hair, her flawless skin, and her belief in herself and her appearance. She knows that the female body is not something to be ashamed of; it's something to be fiercely honored—and moisturized daily.

But now that we've caused feminism to have its moment, we'd like to take the time to tell you how to be feminist in book form! Why? Because you've already met the criteria for being

---

* We LOVE men!

a better feminist than everyone else: you're a woman,* you can read,** and you buy things. The rest of feminism is a piece of cake.

Still confused about feminism? It's actually very simple. The first rule of feminism is to *Get it, girl,* but first we must get to know the ladies who paved the way and *got it* before you.

You probably didn't know this, but feminists have been around since before "feminism" was even a twinkle in Rosie's rivets. Women had "Girl Power" before the Spice Girls ever gave it a name. Learning about these brave women*** can inspire us to keep on fighting for what they never had. Think about it. Our great-grandmas couldn't even vote *or* wear pants. Could you imagine living in a world where you couldn't vote or wear pants? You couldn't even vote to wear pants—*because you couldn't vote.* That's just how bad it was, pants-wise, before feminism.

And Grandma? You wouldn't *believe* some of the stuff she wasn't able to do. She probably can't do much now either. Anyway, while Grampa was out getting day-drunk and smoking the cigars he stole off dead Germans, Grandma was staying at home raising your mom, who was a baby, and having lots of other babies as well. You think 77 cents on the dollar is bad? Try getting paid in babies!

See how much progress we've made already? Okay, history lesson almost complete.

So your mom—sorry, we know you guys aren't talking right now and don't want to make it weird, but hear us out. Mom was probably working while you were growing up, looking for a crack in that glass ceiling, so you could break it with your sweet new position as a social-media marketing manager! Without Mom (sorry, this is the last mention, we promise; we know she was never around for you emotionally and you deserve to tell her how you feel), and without her brave and creative use of shoulder pads, you wouldn't be where you are now. So thanks, Mom! (Sorry!!!!!)

Today, plenty of women are walking around being feminist left and right like it's no big deal, and they *don't even know it.***** Our duty is to vlog, pin, and tweet about feminism as much as we can until every woman —male or female—is touched by the angel of feminism.

In order for you to understand the feminism of today, let's take a step back and look at a brief history of feminism from the beginning.

---

* Or a guy! Men, mmmm.
** You friggin' KILL at reading!!!
*** And also men! We can't forget the men!
**** Taylor Swift, we're looking at you! So glad you finally joined the party. You so pretty!

OFFICIAL TIMELINE OF FEMINISM

The institution of marriage begins. "Wife" replaces "concubine." Progress!
8000 B.C.E.

Jesus was a feminist and didn't even know it! (He wore sandals and loved potlucks and wine.)
0

Mulan does her thing in the East.
620

Beyoncé's father, Mathew Knowles, is born, and also bell hooks.
1952

Men let us vote! Still kind of enslaved, though.
1920

Dr. Quinn, medicine woman, becomes the first female doctor (and constantly asks herself whether her career is getting in the way of her ability to be a good mother).
1860s

Betty Friedan writes *The Feminine Mystique*. Peggy Olson becomes the first woman in a high-powered position in advertising.
1963

Beyoncé is born!
1981

Murder, She Wrote shows that women can solve crimes too!
1984

Hillary Clinton, we guess . . .
1993

Beyoncé turns five!!
1986

Geraldine Ferraro becomes the first female vice-presidential candidate to run for a major party in the United States.
1984

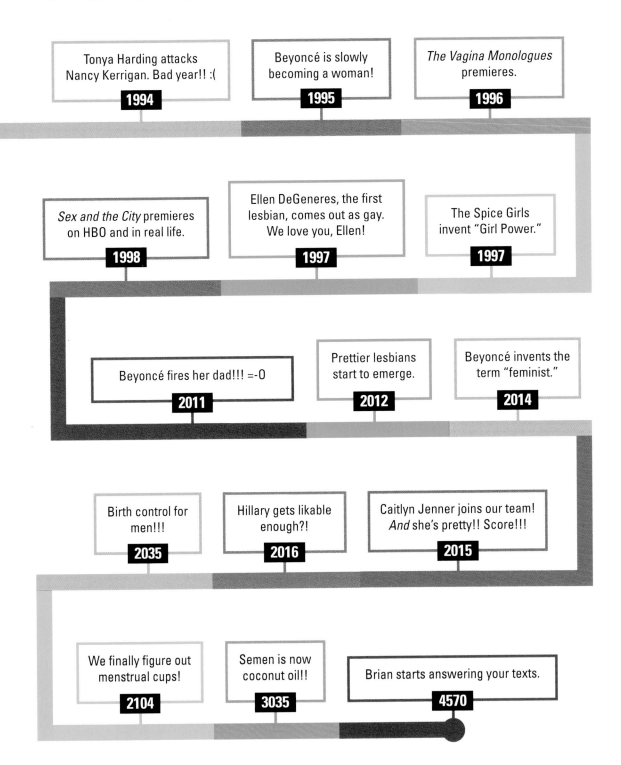

Tonya Harding attacks Nancy Kerrigan. Bad year!! :(
1994

Beyoncé is slowly becoming a woman!
1995

The Vagina Monologues premieres.
1996

Sex and the City premieres on HBO and in real life.
1998

Ellen DeGeneres, the first lesbian, comes out as gay. We love you, Ellen!
1997

The Spice Girls invent "Girl Power."
1997

Beyoncé fires her dad!!! =-O
2011

Prettier lesbians start to emerge.
2012

Beyoncé invents the term "feminist."
2014

Birth control for men!!!
2035

Hillary gets likable enough?!
2016

Caitlyn Jenner joins our team! *And* she's pretty!! Score!!!
2015

We finally figure out menstrual cups!
2104

Semen is now coconut oil!!
3035

Brian starts answering your texts.
4570

So there you have it. We've come a long way, but we have so much more to do before the metaphorical *V* is truly equal to the metaphorical *D*. 'Cause let's face it: the literal *V* is absolutely *nothing* like the literal *D*! Here's why.

DICK VS. VAGINA

DICK	VAGINA
Has three smells: washed, unwashed, cursed	Has at least 27 different smells
Is usually 3 to 7 inches	Is usually 0 inches because it's a hole
Increase in size valued societally	Increased width over time not valued societally
Definitely ejaculates	Does *not* ejaculate, no matter what Karen keeps saying
Goes in holes	*Is* a hole

Even though we're no longer smoking two packs a day and sneaking Schnapps to survive a lifetime of housewifery, we still have so much more to do to improve the world for women. From day to night to the morning-after pill, feminism is a work in progress, and you have the power to shape it—with the help of us, a women's magazine that is now also a book!*

With the right tools and a dependable moisturizing routine, you too can be a beautiful, strong feminist. Heck, you probably are right now and don't even know it! But you better read this book just to make sure, because there are a lot of things you are probably doing wrong. It's okay, girlfriend! Nobody's perfect.**

We're so glad you've decided to join us on this feminist journey through the femwilderness as we reach toward the white light of femquality. Do bring sunscreen. Do bring a bottle of water and a high-protein snack. But please do not bring Jen. We don't have time to listen to her shit right now. Now let us embark upon our odyssey through womanity!

You may have heard some ladies refer to *feminisms,* as in, "There is more than one type of feminism." And they're right! Feminism is multifaceted, with women of many different

---

* Which was a lot harder to write than a magazine, btw. Our editor said we couldn't include four chapters on Rihanna's Instagrams.

** Except Beyoncé.

backgrounds and privileges working together for equality. Although there are several types of feminists, most feminists fall into one of two camps: Beyoncé and Taylor Swift. Your journey begins with one core decision, a decision you cannot undo once it is made; once you decide to be feminist, you need to know which of these two feminists you're going to be. To help you decide, here are some definitions we pulled straight from a book (it's our book; we wrote it).

TAYLOR VS. BEYONCÉ

TAYLOR SWIFT FEMINISM

Doesn't kiss and tell; is very pretty, with symmetrical features and a flawless upper midriff; always caters to the little people, and is never seen in public without a bold red lip.

Is heavily influenced by the early Lena Dunham feminists; takes a strong feminist stance by talking mostly about dating and heartbreak.

TSFs devote significant amounts of time to decorating themselves with pretty girlfriends in order to show that they support other women.

BEYONCÉ FEMINISM

Supports the unadulterated liberation of women from men while also embracing their sexuality, while also embracing marriage, while also embracing taking their husband's last name, while also embracing having sex in a bathtub.* Hey, we never said feminism wasn't complicated!

Bey Fems have no problem admitting they are feminist and display their political aims via impeccable and luscious thighs as well as big glowing signs that say "FEMINIST."

Which kind of feminist are *you*? Write it in the comments! Oh, there's no comments section in this book? Well, we're still learning how this whole book thing works. Okay, just write it down on a piece of paper, attach it to a dove, and say your wish three times as you release the dove into the world. That way, you will for sure become a feminist! Good luck!

---

* SERFBORT!!! Lol, remember???

Plinky the Fairy Witch

Luck you'll need, yes, luck times three.
You'll need pluck and you'll need me!
I'm Plinky the Fairy Witch, enchanté!
I guide new feminists on their way!

So follow me, child, and hear my spell.
I'll guide you through book club, and
    potlucks, and hell.
For stresses will stress, and pressure will presh,
When you're a "FEMINIST" with a
    capital F!

Tee hee! Too hoo!
Follow me, little you!
I once robbed a bank in Kalamazoo!

 DISCLAIMER

Plinky is a second-wave feminist fairy who was trapped in a tampon dispenser at Lilith Fair for twenty years. We think she's making that bank-robbery thing up, because she doesn't seem like the type. There is a chance that she's a dangerous radical, but for our purposes please try to ignore that. She has a lot of great things to say aside from the crime stuff, which, again, is probably not true. Just FYI!

HOW TO FEMINIST

Beyoncé

Repeat the following out loud, whenever you're in need of wombspiration, whether you're getting catcalled on the street or about to undertake a spiritually exhausting day of shopping.

We are the hands of the Goddess, Beyoncé,
And to her we offer to put our hands up.

We are the booties of the Goddess,
And to her we offer up cake by the pound.

We are the moufs of the Goddess, Bae,
And to her we offer cigars on ice.

The patriarchy:
How the hell did this shit happen?
Oh, babeh.

Let us find strength
In this kitchen half-naked.
In her name we make the world ready
For this jelly.

HOW TO FEMSPLAIN FEMINISM TO YOUR FRIENDS

Feminism is all about us women having each other's backs, but it's also about setting an example for those who may not be as enlightened as yourself. After all, you're not really a feminist unless you're sharing a slice of feminism with all your gal pals and raising them up to your level.* Since a rising tide lifts all boats, it's up to you to gath-her your friends together for gal-therings from time to time, braid their hair into cute feminist plaits, and empower them with the feminist discussions and tools they need in order to know that you already know more than they do. That's what feminism is all about!

You may have heard the term "mansplaining," which is when men explain things you already know in a condescending way. Now, when we need to explain important feminist concepts like brow shaping to women (who should probably already know them by now), we "femsplain." Femsplaining allows us to empower ourselves and other women at the same time, while throwing just a teensy bit of shade their way for being so basic. It's a very important part of the work we do!

When you femsplain feminism to your friends, make sure you don't femsplain what's *wrong with other women;*** rather, femsplain what's *right about you.**** If other women come across as lesser feminists as a result, then so be it. It's in your power to feminspire women to be good feminists—almost, but never quite as good as you. Here's how.

Feminvite them over.

A good invite is fun and playful while also conveying the importance of the gal-thering. Use some empowering phrases to get friends excited for the event, like, "We have *got* to get our gal on!" Give the night a fun and funky title like "Lisa's Lady Bash" or "Wear Your Stretchy Jeans!" And always, *always* mention there will be booze. Drinking propels feminist discussion, so pick up your fave bottle of alc-her-hol and get ready to partake in the discourse.

Put on some fempowering music and talk about your bodies.

When your friends arrive, start slow by playing some early Beyoncé and then pass out some homemade probiotic yogurt. This will help get them comfortable and set the mood before

---

* Just under your level, technically, since you knew about feminism first and will always be ahead of them on the curve.
** I.e., that they don't support other women. :-(
*** I.e., how much you support other women. :-)

you dish out that feminist knowledge. Before they know it, you'll be telling them how "real" their bodies are and how beautiful their curves look. In the 1960s, this type of group discussion was called "consciousness raising," but for our modern-day purposes we'd rather call it "woking up like this" because it just sounds better.

Anyway, have your friends sit in a circle and repeat the phrase "I woke up like this" until they start to believe it. Once they start nodding, smiling, and taking their first shaky yet empowered selfies, you'll know they're ready to absorb the lessons that they were not permitting themselves to take in before you came into their life and allowed them to be who they already are.

Literally bake a feminist cake and dish it out to your femfriends.

Baking is fun and a great way to show friends you feel strongly about something (think birthdays, bake-sale fund-raisers). A chocolate cake says, "This cake is for women. Women love chocolate. I feel strongly about that."

If your friends are watching their waistlines and refuse your feminist cake, go ahead and put on your "Fempowerment" playlist. Right as that old Meghan Trainor song comes on, tell them how much "real women" eat cake these days and then reoffer the cake. *Do not let them leave without eating some cake. This is an important step.*

Before you know it they'll be, like, "How do I get this recipe? This dish is so good!" This will allow you to discuss the ins and outs of modern feminism and explain, "Actually, this cake was baked by a man. *The* man." That's where this book comes in. Pass around copies of the book as feminist party favors and get that party started.

Distribute this femiglossary.

When you're part of a movement, particularly a movement that involves women, it's important to have a shared language to discuss your collective experiences and goals as well as common cultural reference points to empower each other with and shout supportively at each other during hard workouts. Whether you're complaining about an uncomfortable bra or petitioning Sony Pictures for more movies with erotic male dancers, expand your her-cabulary and teach your friends about feminism by sprinkling your language with the following terms.

FEMIGLOSSARY

ADVISE-HER: Your role as a feminist, should you choose to take it. From now on, you'll be advising your female friends at every turn. Think of yourself as a life coach and image consultant combined!

ALC-HER-HOL: The most important ingredient for any feminist gal-thering. *Example:* "Did you bring the alc-her-hol?" "What?"

BEYONCÉ: The first feminist.

BEYSCIPLE: A young feminist in training. She can only wake up like this from a nap.

People will listen to almost anything if you can do a solid braid!

CONSCIOUSNESS BRAIDING: Braiding a fellow feminist's hair and raising her up through a sleek and fashionable coif. Such a hairstyle should make her feel sexy, but also allow her to operate machinery or perform surgery, just like a man would.

FEMHIVE: The army of feminists on the Internet, with an arsenal of hashtags at their disposal. *Example:* "Some troll is body-shaming Dana's DIY anal bleaching vlog! #Release the #femhive! #Yesallfemhives."

FEMINISMGASM: A feminist orgasm; can be physical or political. *Example:* "Paul went down on me while we watched a YouTube video of a Michelle Obama commencement speech, which gave me my strongest feminismgasm ever!"

FEMINISTIFY: To be a feminist while also being sexy and beguiling.

GAL-FIRMATION: An affirmation you give yourself when you look in the mirror in the morning that helps you tackle your day as a woman. *Examples:* "At the end of this day is a bottle of wine." "We can do this, uterus." "The longest journey begins with a single step—in heels."

GENDER STUPIDITY: The completely boneheaded ideas some people have about gender. *Examples:* "Men are better than women." "Quilting your feelings is women's work."

HERFBORT: Your vibrator and number-one D alternative when your man's not supporting your feminist goals. *Example:* "I'm so effing horny, but David's seeing that Skrillex cover band with his friends tonight, so I'm gonna have to hop on my herfbort."

HERSHTAG: A hashtag strong enough for a man, but *made for women. Example:* "I'm live-tweeting my natural water birth at 3 P.M. EST! Follow the hershtag #sarahsnaturalwaterbirth for updates. Fingers crossed!!"

INT*HER*NALIZED SEXISM: Internalizing the myths and stereotypes of femininity, processing them, and reclaiming them as our own. *Example:* "Yes, I'm a housewife, but I prefer the term 'stay-at-home bitch,' thank you very much."

MAID-DEN: Like a man cave, but for women. Instead of video games, you can knit, do crosswords, or just gab here. Feel free to decorate it the same way you decorate the rest of your house because that's your job! Fun!

MALE GAYZE: That judgy yet supportive look you get from your gay best friend, who would never objectify you, but will definitely tell you how your boobs look in that V-neck romper.

MASSAGE-ONY: The completely inadequate massages some men offer in return for our ameeezing massages. Equal pay for equal play!

NOT-GUILTY PLEAS*HER*S: Pleasures that only women like (chocolate!), which the patriarchy has made us feel guilty about for that reason. But no longer will we tolerate this guilt inducement! Sorry not sorry! <— Also a good *her*shtag; see above.

PATRIARCH-D: That big ol' sweet, sweet D that keeps you enslaved to the patriarchy.

PRIVILEGE: Not super sure, but your friend Jen keeps asking you to "check" it. Sorry, Jen, we mostly use Venmo!

SHOPAHOL-ETTE: Not an addict (see also: not-guilty pleas*her*s). *Example:* "I'm a shopahol-ette. I just bought eleven copies of the Reductress book for my friends, and I do not feel guilty about that."

SQUAD GOALS: Achievements that you and your girls must accomplish together or you will all have failed. *Example:* Attaining the exact same body type so you can all share outfits!!!

#WCIWCW (WOMEN CRUSHING IT ON WOMAN-CRUSH WEDNESDAY): Like a normal woman-crush Wednesday, but when your woman crush is really crushing it in her chosen field and/or brow game. Don't worry, this woman crush is totally platonic, and you don't have to be a lesbian to do it or to crush it. But as a feminist you totally can be a lesbian if you're into that! Swoon! *Example:* "I'm really proud of all the #WCIWCW who bought the Reductress book."

WOMBVERSATION: Talking with another woman in hushed tones while placing your hands on each other's bellies and speaking your truth.

Gal-therings are a great time to drink alc-her-hol, light wo-tive candles, and have deep wombversations.

WO-TIVE CANDLE: A candle that helps you get in touch with your inner goddess, ideally lit during a full moon or at the time of ovulation.

"YAAAS MEANS YAAAS, QUEEN!": Something to shout at another woman when she is giving enthusiastic consent to a man.

YOU-T-HER-US: Your body, your decision, your uterus! Hands off, men—unless we ask for a nice premenstrual you-t-her-us massage!

IS IT FEMINIST? (A CHART)

Some say feminism is more a theory, but we like to think of it as a label that can be slapped onto or removed from anything we choose. So the next time you're about to see a movie, read a book, or buy a bag of fat-free popcorn, ask yourself: Is it feminist? For your reference, here's a sample guide to what is and isn't feminist.

FEMINIST	NOT FEMINIST
Painting your nails for you	Painting your nails for him
Erotica	Porn
Your vibrator	His dick
Dark chocolate	Milk chocolate
C-sections	Vaginal births
Sexting	Texting
Whoopi Goldberg	Whoopee cushions
Bubble baths	Oatmeal baths
Life Savers	Candy canes
Moesha	Brandy
Oysters	Pearls
Body wash	Soap on a rope
Books	Spicy trail mix
Dance	Magicians
Plastic applicators	Lice
"Whoopee!" (exclamation)	"Makin' whoopee" (sex)
The moon	The sun
Magic Mike	*Magic Mike XXL*
The pill	Condoms
Death by chocolate	The death penalty
Yogurt	Go-Gurt
Having it all	Having a ball

FEMINIST	NOT FEMINIST
Fifty Shades	Of Grey
Tacos	Burritos
Feelings	Facts
Tigers	Lions
Oakland A's	San Francisco Giants
Spinning	Cycling
Coughing	Sneezing
Having a stroke	Burning toast
Bell's palsy	Lyme disease
"Hi."	"Hello."
Pissing	Peeing
Tote bags	Other kinds of bags
Riding a horse	Eating meat
Herb gardens	Electrical fires
Knowing CPR	Being an EMT
Punching	Kicking
"Mmm!"	"Yum!"
Standing	Sitting
Almonds	Peanuts
Coconut milk	Actual milk

THE MANY WAVES OF FEMINISM

As we've explained, feminism didn't just come about all at once. It came in ripples, much like finger curls gracefully draped across time. In other words, it came in waves.

Whether they're beach waves, hair waves, or feminist waves, *we fucking love waves.* So we did a ton of research on feminist waves and discovered that each era had its own style and attitude. Much like New Wave or deciding to wave or not wave at your coworkers outside of work, many women had different ideas about what feminism meant to them, and sometimes it got contentious. For example, many women still wonder today if the five different Spice Girls really did represent *all* women. Fortunately we resolved that question years ago,* so now we can focus on more important questions like, "Will unlikely animal friendships end racism?" and "Is beach hair inclusive?"

Of course, there is no way you will ever win at feminism without knowing *how* each wave of feminism came to pass. And although women throughout history have made lil' feminist steps like winning the right to vote and own property, it's not a cohesive movement until cute catchphrases and songs become associated with the changes. These are what help us to really understand what feminism is about *in this very moment*. After years of research and also just kind of guessing, here are the waves of modern feminism.

THE WAVES OF FEMINISM: TIMELINE

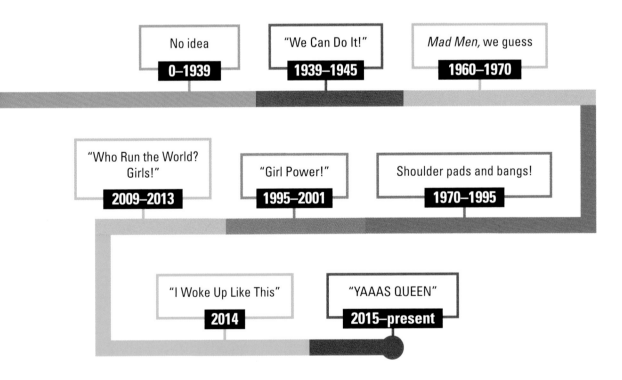

No idea	"We Can Do It!"	*Mad Men,* we guess
0–1939	1939–1945	1960–1970

"Who Run the World? Girls!"	"Girl Power!"	Shoulder pads and bangs!
2009–2013	1995–2001	1970–1995

"I Woke Up Like This"	"YAAAS QUEEN"
2014	2015–present

---

* Of course they do.

0–1939: No Idea

Pass!

1939–1945: The "We Can Do It!" Wave

When Rosie the Riveter took a selfie and captioned it "We Can Do It!" she *literally broke* whatever was around before the Internet. Finally, we had a woman with a catchphrase and a dope outfit that celebrated *us,* which started the "We Can Do It!" wave of feminism. The "We Can Do It!" wave was steadfast in reminding American women that not only can we *do* it; we can look hella *good* doing it, too.

Unfortunately, while a lot of women thought Rosie's "it" meant "we can do anything we set our minds to," a lot of men thought it meant "we can do more work on top of our existing housework." All of this actually made it a pretty stressful time to be a woman. This period brought us an age of killer blue rompers and permission to touch the weights at the gym, but we women soon realized we needed a better solution to gain equality.

Later on, the birth of the first female superhero, Wonder Woman, gave rise to the belief that not only could women fight evil, but they could do it all in a killer outfit while showing off some major cleave. This unfortunately caused a lot of women to immediately feel bad about their newly purchased romper-and-handkerchief getup and get motivated to start making newer and better strides in how good women could look.

1960–1970: *Mad Men,* We Guess

This is the wave where your mom did stuff in an office, also known as the *Mad Men* wave of feminism. Some complicated shit went down somewhere between civil rights and the

Vietnam War. Fortunately, most of it can be figured out by watching *Mad Men,* asking your mom what happened, or just asking your mom what happened on *Mad Men.*

1970–1995: Shoulder Pads and Bangs!

This was when strong women like Mary Tyler Moore, Laverne and Shirley, and Murphy Brown entered the workforce, and the real world has never been the same since. Not only were they the first women to ever be in skilled leadership professions; they skillfully demonstrated the rise and fall of shoulder pads. These brave women showed us that women can do any job a man can do, just as long as she skips to that job while singing or throwing her garments into the air. Also, Murphy Brown showed us that you can have a baby even if you aren't married—talk about DIY!!! These women are real women and not just characters, so if any of them are reading this book, we thank them for kicking feminism up a notch!!!

WHAT DID YOUR MOM DO BEFORE FEMINISM?

"I was fired from my first job for not being 'attractive enough' to be a secretary. Thirty years later, I watched one episode of *Mad Men* and realized why."

"My family forced me to give up the baby I had out of wedlock. A few decades later, *Mad Men* came out, and I realized I should have been focusing on my career all along!"

"Would you look at that Jon Hamm? He's so handsome. Is he single? What a cute butt! Can't you just send him an e-mail or something? I'm dying soon."

1995–2001: "Girl Power!"

This was the wave of feminism that changed feminism forever. "Girl Power!" was the battle cry of the tiny pink spaghetti-strap tops of our youth, and the message was clear: no matter what challenges we faced in modern society, we ruled, and that was that. The Spice Girls came up with this pivotal phrase out of the blue one day, just hanging out together like the best friends forever that they have always been. Plenty of girls already believed that they ruled,* but a lot of them lacked the actual power to carry it out in their daily lives. When the Spice Girls uttered the phrase, "Girl Power!" with their strong, diverse girl fists in the air, the world changed *overnight*.

Now, not only could we yell about how we can "do it"; we could yell about *power,* which was a huge change from what the previous generations were yelling. Finally, the world would know what we wanted, what we really, really wanted.

2009–2013: "Who Run the World? Girls!"

The women's movement made major strides in this era, where we went from being full-time baby ovens to literally *running the world*. Now, with Beyoncé as our figurehead and Michelle Obama as our arms, there was literally no stopping us (girls) from running shit.

Several more feminist issues were left unresolved during this era like, "Can women play video games?" and "Can women wake up . . . like this?" but fortunately these questions would be resolved in the coming wave of feminism.

2014: "I Woke Up Like This"

Sure, we run the world, but many begged the question, "How did we wake up?" And the answer was right in front of us. "Women of the world, you woke up," Beyoncé said, "like *this*." Whatever *this* was, women woke up that way, and there was literally no stopping us from doing it. This not only affirmed our power over the world, but declared that, like Beyoncé, we all naturally wake up looking like goddesses, even before our vitamin B-12 gummy or pits-only shower. We finally took back the A.M. Whose morning? *Our morning!*

---

* The proto-girl-power movement was thought to have begun with the adage "Girls rule, boys drool."

2015–present: "YAAAS QUEEN"

Started by one of our drag-queen sisters, YAAAS QUEEN is an inclusive phrase of affirmation of one's looks or behavior, that set the stage for the next big wave in feminism. The long-term effects and changes of YAAAS QUEEN are yet to be examined, but they seem to champion the looks and works of women who are not Beyoncé.

And there you have it: the long, slow arc of feminist history. Whether you're a feminist or just a woman interested in looking at feminism, it's important to understand what our foremothers did to shape the feminist world we enjoy today, one brave wave at a time.

CELEBS ON BEING FEMINIST

Some of our favorite female celebrities are jumping on the feminist bandwagon. You heard it here first (after they told *us*): being a feminist is cool now! As the buzz around feminism grows, everyone's rocking that feminist label.* Here's what these tastemakers had to say when we asked them about coming around to feminism.

Madonna

"I date a lot of younger men, and I recently discovered I can call it feminism."

Oprah

"I am definitely a feminist, yes. But first and foremost, I am Oprah."

Whoopi Goldberg

"Who is this? How did you get this number?"

---

* Feminist Label™, Property of Reductress.

Taylor Swift

"At first I thought being feminist was gross, 'cause who wants to burn cute bras and wipe period blood on their face like war paint? Then I realized both those things would look super cool in a music video, so I'm all over this feminist craze."

Katy Perry

"I wasn't a feminist until people started saying feminists could be sexy, and then it hit me like, yeah, I *am* a feminist. I mean, look at my boobs. I'm really into feminism now and also these cupcake barrettes made by adorable Japanese kids."

Shailene Woodley

"I used to not consider myself a feminist, but now I do. Here, have some of these foraged cricket heads."

Lassie

"I'm actually a boy!"

BOO! THE PATRIARCHY IS A SPOOKY GHOST

You know when you're sitting alone in a room and you feel a cold breeze on your neck that makes you shudder for just a second, and you ask if anybody else felt it, but nobody did? *That's the patriarchy.* The patriarchy is like a spooky ghost. You may not be able to see him, but you can hear him, and he just called you fat.*

---

* Even though you can tell by the sound of his disembodied voice that he's got a total dad bod (which you're actually into, but still).

This ghostly specter whispers in women's ears that *condoms feeeel weeirdd,* and *if you have to get an abortion, that's on youuu.* Every time we look over our shoulders, we feel the chill of the patriarchy telling us *you'd loook better withoouut maakeuup,* but then saying *youuu loook siiick* when we aren't wearing makeup, which is ironic because the patriarchy looks like a fucking ghost.

Since the patriarchy is sneaky and invisible, it also has a way of getting away with stuff that nonghosts usually can't get away with. While actual living men used to be the ones keeping us holed up in the house all day watching soaps and breast-feeding our boring lives away, now the patriarchy does that all without ever being a tangible entity! Think about it: Why does that inner voice saying you're not good enough *sound so spooky?*

Unfortunately, men aren't able to feel the presence of the patriarchy themselves. But as with our periods, some are able to just trust us and believe that it's really happening. This is why we have to trust our feminine sixth sense when we feel that icy dick brush across the back of our neck as we try to ask for a raise and say, "*I see patriarchy.*"

You may have heard people talking about "dismantling the patriarchy," and the reason why it has been so hard is because, like most ghosts, it can slip through your fingers and walk through walls. The only way to end the patriarchy is to acknowledge its presence in the room and to say aloud, "I ain't afraid of no ghost!"

HAZARD: THE PATRIARCH-D

One sneaky tool the patriarchy uses to distract us is the patriarch-D (dick). The patriarchy knows if we get caught up in trying to get that dick, we'll stop paying attention to what the hand in that puppet dick is attached to.

You've probably fallen victim to the patriarch-D and the patriarchy prop-up artists who keep it going at some point in your life. Maybe you're patting yourself on the back for getting so close to that former major league baseball player you matched with on Tinder, when suddenly you realize that you're just one of 107 models he invited to his pool party, and you're about to drink too much champagne before you stumble home dickless.

This happens to all of us, because *the patriarch-D wants to make you feel desperate* and think that you need this, that it is an honor just to be included in this boob medley that will disappear from that shortstop's mind before your Uber even gets you home. Meanwhile you could be having fun in an empowering way, like hanging out in Oprah's castle eating ice cream and rewatching her favorite death moments in *The Hunger Games.* You don't need men to have a good time. In fact, sometimes life is better without the D.

Another example of taking the patriarch-D is when a guy convinces you to go see the latest movie in which adorable sex kittens cling to a nervous and weak baby-man who hangs out with space robots, or a talking stuffed animal, or Jonah Hill. You'll rack your brain trying to discover the character's sex appeal, while your guy assures you he's "the funniest dude alive." The patriarch-D is trying to neg you into thinking *you're* the one who doesn't "get it" if you don't subscribe to the D in all its forms. But your movie dollars don't need to go toward supporting the patriarch-D.

Contrary to what the patriarch-D tells you, you don't have to like movies with titles like *Angry American Shooter Team: Dick's Dawning.* In fact, when you see the trailer and think to yourself, "I will not like this movie," trust your gut and don't see it. Instead, take yourself to a movie of Channing Tatum grinding on some tasteful furniture he just made so you can slurp up that feminist D! Seriously, who needs a hot lady on a car or a hot lady alien on a spacecraft or a hot rabbit in a dress when you can get some Tatum on a mid-century chaise lounge? Feminist D is plentiful; you just have to know where to find it.*

Other places to avoid if you don't want to be assaulted by the patriarch-D and the legion of prop-up artists who wield it include: car washes, social media, higher education, business, inside a baseball hat, and being within earshot of Adam Levine.

---

* E.g., in formerly women-only colleges that now admit men.

Here is the World Watch List of the top-five worst offenders of patriarch-D and how to control yourself in each situation.

5. Your Friend's Cousin

He made out with you in the hot tub that one time and then never answered your instant messages, sending you into an emotional tailspin that lasted until the end of your back-to-school shopping. Make no mistake: that was not the first time he ruined someone's summer. Often going under the aliases of Ryan, Brad, Jackson, or Connor, your friend's cousin is known for totally kissing girls *with tongue* and then going off the grid. He must be stopped. Next time you find yourself in a Jacuzzi as he tries to sneak a peek-a-boob under the water, tell him, "I deserve a man who will respect me inside and outside of this hot tub. Also, I blocked you on AIM."

4. The Supermarket Deli Guy with Frosted Tips and a Barbed-Wire Tattoo

You know the one: he's the hottie all the moms jockey to have slice their turkey—*thick*. Not much is known of his origins, though he was probably a surfer or model at one point. Maybe a body builder or even a landscaper. But now he lives the easy life of slicing cheddar and slaying poon. He's a dangerous mom-sexer who will send all future PTA meetings into a tailspin,* and he must be brought to justice. Instead of subjecting yourself to his slutty salami, head over to the fish guy, who will appreciate you for who you are on the inside, because you're the first woman who has ever smiled at him.

3. That Bartender Who Looks Like Jon Hamm (and Knows It)

You asked him, "Does anyone ever tell you you look like Don Draper?" He feigns surprise and says, "Ha! Wow, you think so?" *Do not* fall for this. He's been doling out subpar finger-bangs ever since *Mad Men* debuted. There's nothing worse than a guy who knows he looks like an unattainably suave celeb, so keep your distance. He's not worth staying out late five nights a week. Trust us. To avoid that dick-laden heartache, try dating a guy who looks more like Vince Vaughn.

---

* These meetings were a mess to begin with, but that doesn't excuse him from adding fuel to the fire.

2. Dan, with the Hat

Fucking Dan. Ugh. With the hat. I mean, seriously? Stay away from Dan. Stupid Dan. Fuck Dan and his hat. Who does he think he is? Just because he has a hat we're supposed to be all over his dick? Yeah right. Yeah right. No way, Dan. No one cares how cute you are in that hat. Ugh. Stupid hat.* Simple solution: stay away from hat.

1. Your Ex Who Had a Twin Bed

It's not about the size of the boat, but the motion of the ocean—and that ocean was more like a puddle. Sure he has a gorgeous D and a propensity to make coffee in the morning, but your neck has still not recovered from spending the night in a child-size bed. Ignore the love you once felt and focus on the pain you felt while sleeping in a *Z* shape. Still, this is the most sinister of all the patriarch-Ds. You think, "Maybe he's changed. Maybe he got a full." But don't be fooled: this oppressor will never, *ever* buy a bed frame. Stay back. Move forward. Bring him to justice. Burn his mattress and never look back.

HOW TO BE FEMINIST WITHOUT BEING TOO "OPINIONY"

Now that you've read our beautiful words, you know feminism is the best. But please, puh-leeze, don't give feminism a bad name by being all crazy about it. Look, we've worked too hard to make this club shiny and fun and discreet. We didn't invite you to the party to blow up our spot. When a woman openly shares an opinion, she is often viewed as angry or "reactionary." You don't want us to get flagged by men as annoying or unlikable, do you? So here's how to have legitimate feminist thoughts without being too "in your face" about it and giving feminism a bad look.

First, don't *ever* make a man take direct responsibility for his acts of misogyny, okay? *Be chill!* Guys love when women are chill. They are chill most of the time, so get on their level! If you do have to make a point, use vague terms to describe what the actions of an evil sexist bogeyman might look like, so he knows it's definitely not him you're talking about. Hopefully, over time, the men in your life will start to absorb this knowledge, and it will be reflected in their own future behaviors. This may take a really long time, but it's definitely worth avoiding an argument tonight, because he seems really tired right now and you don't want to stress him out.

---

* Is he single, though?

OPINIONY: *Getting angry*
CHILL: *Journaling!*

Journaling has been a great hobby for women throughout herstory because of its unobtrusive nature. *Men can accept that women are emotional creatures affected by their surroundings as long as women express those emotions privately. It's not nagging if it's on paper and that paper never sees the light of day. So just journal about how his statements about how "pussy tastes weird" made you feel.**

OPINIONY: *Feeling disempowered*
CHILL: *Decorating!*

If a guy sees empowerment as "some dumb woman thing" or an act of insecure desperation, it will fit well within his idea of your role as a woman and won't upset the tried-and-true gender dynamic he loves so dearly. Men aren't as offended by feminist ideals when they're presented subtly, right under their noses, in the guise of being things other than self-respect. So get craftin'! Frame a cute print containing Rubenesque figures to remind yourself of body positivity. Find a piece of reclaimed wood and paint the word "HOME" on it to renew your sense of rugged feminine individuality. He'll shrug it off as some romantic "Pinterest bullshit." But you'll know. And you'll respect yourself, even if your life partner doesn't.

---

* Recorded herstory didn't begin until we were allowed to learn to read and occasionally own small amounts of paper, the dates for which are kinda fuzzy, but we *do* know we came out of the gate running with the journaling thing due to lots of pent-up emotions.
** Pretty bad!!!!

OPINIONY: *Being silently furious*
CHILL: *Becoming a model!*

You can be a feminist and still be sexy! All you need is a five-foot-nine, 110-pound frame and to be under the age of twenty-two. Be fierce but silent, like a sexy androgynous robot that men want to have space sex with—this is your best chance at making men care about your feelings and listen to your opinions! Not qualified to be a professional model?[*] Take some super-beautiful selfies. Women who are conscious of their flawless appearance do not seem like angry old hags trying to upset the delicate balance of men's cultural dominance.

OPINIONY: *Being misunderstood*
CHILL: *Writing some poetry!*

If there's one thing most people can say about poetry, it's that they don't "get it" and aren't paying any attention to it. Sound familiar? That's just like women and feminism, which is why feminism and poetry go hand in hand! Nod to the patriarchy in subtle nuanced prose or add some verse to spice it up. Bust out some spoken-word floetry about how independent you feel when you squeegee your own windshield at the gas station. When you can be feminist without being disruptive—and sound pleasantly lyrical at the same time—everybody wins![**]

---

[*] Why did God make you five foot eight?! WHY!!??!
[**] Poetry is basically the only reason Emily Dickinson wasn't burned at the stake. Win!

OPINIONY: *Trying to compete with men*
CHILL: *Doing a crossword puzzle!*

What better way to assert your intelligence as a woman than by conquering the dominion of a gridded word game? Take that, patriarchy! Take that, Will Shortz!* The men around you will be none the wiser about how equal you are to them in mental faculties while your feminist spirit rages in the back pages of the newspaper. What's a five-letter word that this activity isn't? P-u-s-h-y.

OPINIONY: *Having a long conversation about what your life has been like as a woman*
CHILL: *Hosting a book-club meeting!*

The beauty of the book club is that no man would dare set foot in one, so you're free to whisper about the unfairness of your male coworker's promotion or the ways Fifty Shades of Grey made you feel things without upsetting your husband in the other room. Get wine-drunk and drunk on feminism in this empoweringly secret environment, free from male sovereignty.

OPINIONY: *Lecturing him on body acceptance*
CHILL: *Taking a dance class!*

If you liked the freedom of the book club, but can't sit still, you'll love dance class. Strutting your body all over the room is a great way to say to a small group of female and possibly gay male strangers: "Real women have curves!" "Take back the night!" "Women!" and "Oh no, the barf, it's up coming again." Yay dance class!

* Seriously tho, we love you boi!

OPINIONY: *Yelling*

CHILL: *Drinking tea!*

Nothing supports and soothes a woman's soul like a good cup of tea. So slide that bra out yo' sleeve (in the privacy of your own home), sit back on the ol' fut', and sip on that good strong-but-sweet feminist chai. And when he just doesn't get why you "can't just take a joke," a relaxing organic rooibos tea can help you meditate on why you've stayed in this relationship for so long without starting to hate yourself and doubt your feminine power. Getting in touch with the simple, soulful pleasures of being a woman reminds you that being a woman is not a bad thing, while also leaving him alone for once!

OPINIONY: *Banging your head against the wall in a desperate cry for help*

CHILL: *Joining a roller derby team!*

Do you like feminist exercise, but are more violent than graceful? You might be a derby girl! Roller derby is a great way to get together with your strong but still heavily lipsticked gal pals for a little competitive fun. What's more feminist than knocking other girls out of the way, possibly causing serious injury, so your besties can get slingshotted ahead for points? Bonus: men will love it because they can watch it like a real sport, but there are girls with booty shorts on. You're tricking men into being feminists! Double win! Points! Go team! So much blood!

Feminism is so, so, so fun. But nothing puts the brakes on that fun like a man walking in the room and being all, "What is going *on* in here?" In the event that your feminist activities are discovered, quick diversions include bursting into song, asking him how to fix something in the room, and fainting.

BAD FEMINISTS (A LIST)

Not all feminists are created equal. Unfortunately, some feminists distract from the real causes (women being strong *and* beautiful) with lesser, more boring causes (women in STEM).* As important as it is to model ourselves after the good feminists out there,** it's equally vital to separate ourselves from the bad feminists—the ones who give feminism a bad look.

Bad feminists make feminism look like something to fall asleep to, like your mom droning on about how she does all the cleaning around here. Good feminists make feminism look hot, exciting, and fun, like an HBO series starring a cast of four different (but not *too* different) female friends who all get laid from time to time or a music video in which pretty girls act tough or pretend to be ugly. Bad feminists make all feminists look bad, which is why we have to call them out on our Tumblr, like, every other day.

Now that we've won the right to vote, we feminists need to focus on the more relevant issues at hand, like being sex positive, feeling fierce during sex, and showing that we women can also have positive feelings about sex. Let's ditch yesterday's issues, like birth control, equal pay, and "women in leadership" (whatever that means!), and move our cause forward. And while we're at it, let's ditch these bad feminists who are holding us back.

Hillary Clinton

Sure, she puts women's rights at the center of her agenda and champions the causes of women all over the world, but unfortunately she is just too darn unlikable and gives feminism a bad look. Her Twitter is whack!*** Maybe instead of cosponsoring a fair-pay act, she could try a bolder shade of lipstick that would make people *want* to see more women in leadership positions? Sorry, Hill, until you turn your vibes around, you're just a bad feminist!

Roxane Gay

She wrote a book called *Bad Feminist*. A bit on the nose, don't you think? Methinks the lady doth protest too *little*. Case closed!

---

* We had a woman doctor once and she was a hella bitch!
** Kisses, Taylor!!
*** Also, Benghazi. (What is Benghazi?)

Angelina Jolie

Jolie works hard as a UN diplomat and philanthropist and bravely shared the story of her double mastectomy, which *technically* could be seen as empowering to other women. But shouldn't she be spending more time on her sorely neglected acting career? Why let that pretty face go to waste when she could be depicting more strong female psychos on-screen? All that humanitarian work takes her away from doing films like *Girl, Interrupted 2: Stop Interrupting Me in This Workplace,* a script we wrote! Angelina, please call us!!

Malala Yousafzai

On the surface, this teen Pakistani activist and Nobel Prize winner *seems* like a good feminist, fighting for her right to an education and rocking a headscarf like no one else. But is she feminist? No, she isn't. You have to be twenty-one in order to be a feminist. That's just the rules. I mean, sure, she continued her campaign for expanding educational opportunities for young girls despite surviving an assassination attempt by the Taliban, but does she know what it's like to be a woman in the workplace who *needs* happy hour? Like, *needs it*?? We think not.

bell hooks

Although hooks has written a lot of great books about feminism and provided some interesting feminist theory, it's just hard for us to imagine that a *real* feminist wouldn't capitalize her own name. C'mon, girl—believe in yourself! You're a great lady writer!! For your convenience, here is what your name would look like capitalized: Bell Hooks. Wow! Nice, right?

The next time you're perusing the fare at your local bookstore* and you come across the works of any of these "feminists," think twice before using that gift card. Is this the feminism you want? Is it the feminism you need? Or is it, like, stressing you out? Frankly, our version of feminism involves a little less squinting at the page while wrapped in a pile of raggedy throws like a shut-in and a little more dancing on top of a bar while men *and women* cheer. This is what a real feminist looks like!

---

* A.k.a. Amazon.com.

INTERSECTIONALITY IN FEMINISM: FOR WHITE WOMEN!

Are you a straight white female? Okay: Did you know lesbians can also be feminist? And people of color, too? It may seem revolutionary, but all of those groups do contain women. And these days, feminism is for everybody! Even men, occasionally.*

This is what we call *intersectional feminism*. Wait—don't run away! We know it's a big word, but we promise that knowing it is *essential* (also a big word!).

Contrary to popular belief, women who aren't heterosexual, able-bodied, cisgender,** or white might face even more struggles when it comes to gaining equality. A lot to process, we know. But bear with us: intersectional feminism can be just as much fun as regular old feminism! For example, while we're fighting for our right to equal pay in the film industry, we can take a sec to fight to see that minorities get any representation in the film industry whatsoever. That is our solemn duty as feminist allies to our less privileged sisters. Think of being an ally as being a friend who helps her girlfriends bring themselves up to her level, leading by unearned example.

This helps us make a more equal and more inclusive world, which is very on trend right now! Even advertisers are being inclusive these days, which is a great indicator of when something is cool. So hop on the intersectionality train and diversify your feminist goals.

If you're a white woman, you have a lot to fight for, but you also share a lot of the advantages white men have. This is called *privilege* (huh?). Because you have more privilege than a lot of other women, *you must use it for good* and not evil, while also pulling off a killer outfit to show that helping others is cool. We know it's a lot! But we know that you, as a white woman, have the privilege to handle it.

How to Use Your Privilege for Good

Here are some ways you can #checkyourprivilege and help others, while also being an ameeezing ally.

Tell a lesbian that you find another woman attractive.

Nothing assures a lesbian you're on her side like letting her know that you also, theoretically, could be into another woman. Whenever an attractive woman walks by and you're within

---

* When they're fucking a feminist.
** If you don't know what this term means, just know it's referring to you.

earshot of your gay acquaintances, turn to them and say, "Hot, right?!" Feminism is about equal rights for *everyone*.

Say, "I'm not racist!"

Maybe something you said or did was offensive to a person of color. If their feelings were hurt, the best way of comforting them is by letting them know that it was not your intention to offend and that they maybe imagined the whole thing, because you are *not* racist. You don't see color and aren't even that good at figuring out which shade of blue looks best on you. They'll be so relieved to know you're not a racist!

Attack white men.

Nothing puts you squarely on the side of inclusivity like taking jabs at white men at every opportunity. When your coworker Mike leaves the room and you're left with your Pacific Islander coworker Ann, turn to her and say, "Ugh, white guys, amiright?" She'll know you stand in solidarity with her goals, even if she is married to Mike.

Really emphasize your proper pronoun use when talking about a trans person.

Example: "I'm such a big CAITLYN Jenner fan. SHE is so beautiful." No one will doubt your commitment to trans rights now!

Pick their brains.

Inclusivity is all about dialogue. Don't be afraid to pull someone aside and ask, "So what's it like being gay/black/trans/Mexican/different?" They'll appreciate your taking the time to single them out. Also, make sure to use the phrase "pick your brain." People love that!

Tell them you can relate.

If someone from an underrepresented group does start sharing their experiences with you, let them know you sympathize. Say things like, "As a woman, I totally get what it's like." Equating all of our struggles gives us all more power!

Intersectionality for Everyone Else

If you're not a cisgendered white woman, you know that they don't get this ally thing right 100 percent of the time (or even like 60 percent). So we partnered with Noway aspirin to offer this exclusive coupon for ten free aspirin, just for you!* Noway can help you deal with the headache of listening to your monumentally privileged acquaintances say stupid things, like saying that Malcolm X was "way meaner" than Martin Luther King, Jr., or asking what it was like to grow up in a foreign country you have never even been to, or trying to explain why their Halloween costume is okay.

---

* Our legal team tells us that, due to discrimination laws, this coupon will also work for cisgendered white women.

THE NINE CIRCLES OF HELL FOR WOMEN WHO DON'T HELP OTHER WOMEN

Taylor Swift once said, "Katie Couric once said, 'Madeleine Albright once said, "There's a special place in hell for women who don't help other women."'" According to many theologians, she's correct—at least partially. There are said to be *nine* circles of hell specifically designed for women who make social or professional faux pas. Save yourself from eternal punishment by reading this list. You're not on here, are you?

FIRST CIRCLE:
Women who don't participate in group texts

This is Limbo, for women like you who leave everyone hanging. You were specially selected for a hilarious thread about something that pertains to all of you (usually something cray-cray an ex-friend posted on Facebook). You were called upon, and you failed to answer that call. You'll spend forevermore asking strangers if you can borrow their charger.

Notable residents: Estelle Getty, most succubae

SECOND CIRCLE:
Women who post hideous pictures of other women on social media

You're a hot girl with a brand new iPhone, an itchy trigger finger, and no sense of other people's vanity whatsoever. Even if your friend just went through a breakup and needs all the rebound-attracting pics she can get, you'd still post a shot of her mid-yawn, with the caption, "I love my beautiful friend!!!" Your punishment is having large-scale portraits of your weird elbow skin posted online every hour on the hour. Repent!!!!

Notable residents: Cleopatra, your Aunt Jill

THIRD CIRCLE:
Women who bring chips to a potluck

First of all, potluck means cooking. If they wanted to throw a party where everyone bought 7-Eleven chips at the last minute, they'd have called it a "Let's All Give Up" party. Plus, all those who made salsa, hummus, or artichoke dip are *already* bringing chips, so there'll be lots of crunchy waist-killers left over to tempt your host. This is a crime punishable by an eternity of trying to quietly chew something crunchy in a crowded lecture hall.

Notable residents: Mary Todd Lincoln, that girl Jess from work

FOURTH CIRCLE:
Women who never have cash

Unless you have an ATM phobia, there's no excuse for not having at least 20 bucks on you, especially when your ass knows it's brunch o'clock. Your sniveling pleas of "Can I just Venmo you?" and "They take cards, right?" have echoed in businesses everywhere, from scoop shops to Moroccan rug markets. Until the end of time, you'll be forced to split $25 restaurant checks between eight different credit cards. And yes, they're *all* Chase Sapphire. Burn, wench!

Notable residents: Joan of Arc

FIFTH CIRCLE:
Women who play-slap your shoulder way too hard

Ugh, we get it, you're a brassy gal who loves a good laugh. That doesn't give you license to ruin trivia night by dislocating the shit out of someone's shoulder. This circle of hell is full of broads like you, who can't accurately express their laughter without assaulting someone. You'll spend eternity trying to push a boulder up a mountain while TVs everywhere play your least-favorite episode of *Roseanne*.

Notable residents: "Unsinkable" Molly Brown, Gertrude Stein

SIXTH CIRCLE:
Women who cancel at the last minute

There is no girls' night you won't skip, no baby shower you won't "forget" about, and no wingman duty you won't weasel your way out of. Everything you type into your phone autocorrects to "OMG totally forgot, so sorry to back out!!!" Prisoners of this sorry place are doomed to wait at a wine bar alone until the universe folds in upon itself.

Notable residents: Helen of Troy, Nefertiti, Mary Queen of Scots, pretty much all queens

SEVENTH CIRCLE:
Women who only carry applicator-free tampons

Your friend asked if you had a tampon she could use, not, "Hey, do you have a fun excuse for me to finger-fuck myself in this Chili's?" Her polite, confused smile clearly means, "I'm now going to shove a wad of toilet paper in my underwear. Thanks for nothing," but still, you give her a smug "You're welcome." Your unrepentant earth-friendliness will have you spending the afterlife with bloody fingernails.

Notable residents: Dara S. from your high-school tennis team, Bonnie Parker (of Bonnie and Clyde)

EIGHTH CIRCLE:
Women who claim to be "still full"

Look, we all do adorable things so that guys will have sex with us. We sing beautiful songs, we volunteer with the elderly, we even bleach our buttholes. But it's too low of a blow to start rhapsodizing about your "huge lunch." That shit is *in the past.* We are at a barbecue *right now,* and it is *time to dine.* No woman can compete for D with a girl who's painfully nibbling the corner of a watermelon wedge. You're doomed to be in a long line for plastic cutlery for all time.

Notable residents: Marie Antoinette, that girl Becca from camp

NINTH CIRCLE:
Women who say "Awww!" at you

Your friend mentions something slightly vulnerable: she got through a whole hot yoga class without going into child's pose or is thinking about signing up for Match.com. A nongarbage person would say "Cool!" but you slither into the conversation with the most condescending sound ever: "Awwwwwwwww!" In just one syllable, you have declared: "I am better than you. You are nothing." Your punishment is to be an adult baby, forever and ever. Awww!

Notable residents: Your cousin Nina, Marilyn Monroe, Ursula the Sea Witch

WARNING: CURVES AHEAD

Abandon hope, all ye who enter here—because feminism is hard! This is your last chance to turn back.

You may think that being a feminist is just your current fabulous life with maybe a few more ponytail days, but make no mistake: achieving feminism is a dangerous quest, sort of like *Lord of the Rings*.* Your days will be filled with all sorts of new perils, and some of your favorite things will no longer be acceptable. Choosing to fight the patriarchy is like choosing the red pill over the blue pill, like Neo does in *The Matrix*.** The knowledge you'll acquire can't be unlearned, and you'll be tasked with using it to convert those around you. You can't make a patriarchy-fighting omelet without breaking a few pubic-hair-preference eggs in the process. As Uncle Ben tells Peter Parker in *Spider-Man*,*** "With great power comes great *her*sponsibility."

Here are the perils you'll face once you win feminism.

Knowing About Stressful Things

Being an intersectional feminist**** means starting every day with a hot cup of global-oppression awareness. Once you're aware of the patriarchy, you'll have to know every depressing fact about everything: which chemicals are in our water, how every meat-producing animal gets slaughtered and how much they are aware of what's happening, which mountainous rebel faction is murdering which mountainous rebel faction, how many trees are left in the rain forest and how tall they are, which state legislature is concocting the latest horrible laws, which must-have products are made in the cruelest factories, what the depression rates are for bullies who get bullied by other bullies, and how long we have before the polar ice caps explode. Yikes!

Are you ready to be the girl who knows how many plastic water bottles are floating in the ocean? If not, maybe you're not ready to be the girl who gets equal pay. Think about *that*. If this sounds like too high a price to pay, gift this book to your offbeat younger cousin and go call someone a bitch. It's okay to turn back and not be feminist—for now.

---

* Best dork movie ever!
** Okay, fine. My ex left a bunch of his DVDs at my house, and I was bored.
*** Seriously, Brad, come get your shit.
**** The cool kind!

Having Friends Who Wear Glasses

Marilyn Monroe said it best: "Men don't make passes at girls who make friends with girls who wear glasses." The rest of your squad isn't making the leap with you (they're "not into negativity"), so it looks like you'll have to make some new friends. Well, brace yourself, because some of them might not be able to wear contacts.

Now that you're a feminist, you're not allowed to care about whether or not your friends are hot (but not *too* hot), and that includes girls with sturdy ears and sensitive corneas. Scared yet? Don't worry too much. You'll still have cute friends, since feminists are cute! You're just not allowed to block a girl's number if she insists on putting dangerous glass right next to her beautiful eyeballs, even if her personal choice is totally cock-blocking you at the club. Still, it's not too late to put down your protest sign and head on home.

Hope You Like Cats

It's not like feminists have to go around in burlap sacks and Birkenstocks, but the fact is that you can't be a feminist and not have a cat. Rules are rules! No more will you be able to brag, "I don't even need a lint roller; I'm just a very low-static person." Everything you own will be covered in the fur of woman's best friend. You will not get through the terror of your first no-makeup selfie without a good purr-cuddle with your brain-parasite-carrying kitty cat. And if you have allergies, it's time to get the fuck over yourself. Do you want to be a feminist or not?

Having to Use a Menstrual Cup

Haven't you heard? Using disposable menstrual products is the same thing as hitting a manatee with your speedboat, backing up, and running it over again. Tampons and pads contribute to the waste stream, and as a feminist you'll have to give a shit about the waste stream—or at least know what that is. That means using a DivaCup, which means being cool with dumping a tiny cup of blood into your office sink three to five times a month.

Okay fine, you don't *have* to shove a rubber trumpet mouthpiece up into your ladypiece, but you better have a solid reason why a menstrual cup is not for you. Try, "It's just too big for my tight lil' pussy," or, "I'm making an artistic statement about our country's love affair with cotton." Everyone will get off your jock—for now. Remember, feminism is about choices and whether or not you've made the right one. Are you ready for that? If not, no one will fault you for turning back now. Really. It's fine. We're not being passive-aggressive about it. Go right ahead.

Being Tolerant of Others (Exhausting)

Just because you get to be judgy doesn't mean you get to be intolerant. Feminists have a responsibility to keep an eye on underrepresented groups and make sure their voices are heard, which can be, like, a huge hassle if you're used to focusing on yourself. Are you ready to be aware of the massive privileges you've been handed as a result of colonialism, systematic oppression, and cultural genocide? 'Cause that shit leaves wrinkles. Just sayin'!!!

If all of these hardships seem too high a price to pay, then perhaps feminism isn't for you. Put this book away and go buy some fringy crop tops from a store that uses slave labor. But if you're determined to soldier on, keep reading. Then buy some fringy crop tops from a store that produces in the United States but has a history of mistreating female employees. You're on your way to being a real feminist!

Plinky: Am I Feminist Yet?

You got through part 1! Perhaps you think,
"Am I feminist now, dear little ol' Plink?"
Oh no, my child, there's a river ahead!
Keep rowing, keep going, there's more to
*   be read!*

Gib gib, goob goob,
Keep reading, you boob!
I once put a pipe bomb in a senator's
*   mailbox, but it was the wrong*
*   mailbox.*
Oh my, what a rube!

 DISCLAIMER

Again, we are mostly sure that she's losing her mind and that these are baseless claims. Her braggadocio should not be taken as fact. Just, like, listen to the nice stuff!

FEMINISM: GET THE LOOK!

A FEMINIST INVOCATION OF

"Real" Women

We are the women of Dove®.
We are real.

The women who soar so high on beautiful batwings of arm fat.
We are realer than those skinny bitches.
Because, actually, men like thick women.
Not that this is about men. This is about us loving ourselves.

We dance in our underwear, big bulky undies.
Flying our white grannies as flags of realness.

Plus-size,
Us-size.

Ain't I a woman,
Who can pose with her other curvy friends, laughing in underwear?
Just 'cause I'm big doesn't mean my skin doesn't need moisture.

We have real thighs, real bellies,
Pussies that don't quit, even in a sandstorm.

We slap on that lotion, together, frenzied, happy, laughing.
Oh my goddess, are we women.

Real beauty.
Real women.
(Not actors.)

THE LOOK OF A FEMINIST IS FEELING BEAUTIFUL FROM WITHIN

It's what's on the inside that counts. And what's inside should be a treasure trove of self-love for your outside.

For generations, a woman's worth was based entirely on how she looked. Only one type of body was acceptable, and if you didn't have the goods, you were doomed to a life of spinning wool and conversing with a cornhusk doll in ill-fitting, unflattering clothes. This was a dark time for women—literally, because many of these women were not encouraged to leave the house. These women were also rarely encouraged to moisturize, because society did not deem them worthy of the cause.

That's right, being deserving of moisturizer is a cause. A *worthy* one.*

How did we get to where we are today? Before the inspiring, affirming advertising that celebrates women's bodies, women struggled to love themselves on the inside *and* out. Faced with a world dominated by advertising designed to *keep them down,* women were forced to believe that their outsides were not good enough and that they could only cherish things like their "personality" or their "soul." Fortunately, feminism has caused a revolution, giving us the products and feel-good social experiment videos that let us love our bodies just the way they are!**

Thanks to the brave marketing wizards of today, we now know that women come in all shapes and sizes and require unique body-affirming products to suit their needs. The current wave of feminism encourages us to embrace our looks, no matter *how* we look, as the best and only way to become a better person. Some feminists are calling themselves "contour feminists."*** Contour feminism focuses on highlighting the good parts of oneself and darkening the bad bits. This way, you can *feel* like a good feminist while also *looking* like one.

Contour feminism**** says that you can make up for any shortcomings as long as you're able to *work it* and *be real.* And let's be real—you can't do that without killer heels and a bold lip. So if you have a gap-toothed smile—that's okay! You just have to know how to

---

* What makes a cause worthy? It's simple: anything that generates cash.

** Well, sort of! You're still gonna need products for that.

*** Similar to but not the same as "Spanx feminists."

**** Also not to be confused with "ombré feminism." An ombré feminist is chill with looking like she let her roots grow out, but still paid a lot to make it look like that—also she's, like, only halfway feminist.

work those pearly whites,* girl. And if you have hips, or thighs, or even freckles, that's okay too! You're alterna-hot and there's a whole porn category subset of guys that are into you! Wow! And of course, there's an exfoliating body wash designed exactly for your weirdo bod. Aww!

#Yesallwomen need to feel beautiful—and use a good exfoliating body wash.

You are beautiful—you just don't know it yet. The best way to become a feminist is to recognize and own your beauty. *If you're beautiful and you know it, clap your hands—you're a feminist!*

One of our greatest causes as feminists is to let women know they are beautiful and therefore worthy of all the things men have.** That's why it was important for us to redefine beauty on our own terms (and rediscover it in the most unsuspecting of beauty products), so that everyone can finally, truly feel beautiful *and* know it—even lesbians!*** One of the best ways to feel beautiful is to look beautiful, and you can't do that without a strict moisturizing regimen. What better way to celebrate your curves than to rub lotion onto each and every one of them?

Beauty routines (especially skin care) help women realize how beautiful they are.

Caress those curves. Fondle the folds. Your skin is beautiful! Because it's supple and smooth now, just like a thin person's skin, even though it's not that. It's *better*. Feminism has many looks. But the most important look is *how you feel on the inside.*

Knowing you're beautiful is the first step to letting everyone else know they're beautiful too. This is our solemn duty, and one of the keys to winning feminism. Winners never quit, and neither do their bodies or their own affirmations of their bodies. Now get out on the field (or on your social-media platform of choice) and start telling everyone that *they're beautiful too.*

---

* And make sure you get them bleached white. Like, super white.

** Or at least help them get a man, so that they'll finally believe us when we say they're beautiful.

*** Lesbians can be beautiful too! Hi, lesbians!

FEMINIST SKIN CARE

Being a feminist doesn't mean you can let your skin go to hell! You're now the face of a movement, so you better make sure that face looks amazing. After all, when you wear your "This is what a feminist looks like" T-shirt, you don't want people to think, "Oh, I see. Feminists look tired."

IN THE AM:

When you wake, give thanks. Another day has been gifted to you and your combination/oily skin. The best way to approach morning skin care is to think natural. No harsh chemicals, no punishing scrubs, just the earth-based goodness women have trusted for centuries. Here's a basic guide to rising and shining, without that shine showing up on your T-zone:

Fill a basin with hot water from your favorite kettle, perhaps the one you inherited from your beloved grandmother.

While leaning comfortably over the basin, drape a soft linen towel over your head so that it covers the entire tub.

Let the steam gently open your pores. Breathe deeply. *Feel* deeply.

Visualize a positive, happy, balanced day. Visualize a luna moth alighting upon two lovers in a twilit dell. Visualize yourself with perfect skin. Wait five minutes, or until you run out of things to visualize.

IN THE PM:

Darkness has fallen across the land, and you're back in your home, exhausted, bloated, and covered in pollutants. Close the blinds. Lock the doors. Put all your Wi-Fi devices on airplane mode. It's go time. You can finally summon dark forces to effectively freeze your face in time, all under the cover of night. Here's how:

Fill a rectangular aluminum container with research-grade liquid nitrogen. Dip your face into it repeatedly until you can't remember who you are anymore. That's good.

Using steel grit you bought from an industrial supplier with a fake name, blast your cheeks, chin, and forehead. You'll know you're done with this step when you start leaking lymph.

Reach under your kitchen sink, grab whatever cleaning agents are there, and spray them all over your face. Bonus points if you accidently create chlorine gas—it's a real bloat-buster!

Let the chemicals sit until your bones start to show or until the screaming stops. Whose screams are those? Are they your screams?

Show the world your best self by consistently sticking to two skin-care routines, one for daytime and one for nighttime. The morning routine is simple, gentle, and natural, giving you the glow you need to start your day. The evening routine, on the other hand, gives you the preserved look of an ageless trophy wife with the use of harsh chemicals, industrial-strength sandblasters, and demonic texts you can somehow read.

Here's the scoop on skin!

In a small mixing bowl, combine the juice from half a lemon, a nice squeeze of honey, a wandering of coconut oil, and a "voilà!" of overripe banana. Mash together with your fingers, which look just like Grandma Lidia's fingers in that photograph of her wedding day. She was so young then. So beautiful.

Apply the mask to your face for ten minutes, or as long as it takes for the mask to bring back a memory from when you were in utero.

Once the memory plays out, slap the mask off your face with cold, wet hands, just like Grandma Lidia did to herself every morning. She told everyone she was twenty-eight well into her seventies, and they believed her!

Roll on a thin layer of olive oil. We know what you're thinking: "Oil on my face?! But won't I break out?!?" Well, you will with *that* attitude! Your pores will self-regulate throughout the day if you keep a bounce in your step and a song in your heart.

Apply a light facial sunscreen with SPF 30 or above. We love Happy Baby's Sun Baby Moisture for Babies (Target, $49.99).

And of course no morning routine is complete without a smile! Don't worry about the lines—joy is a natural anti-ager! You're finally ready to *face* the day.

Punch yourself in the face. Your cheekbones betrayed you.

Stumble downtown to the dumpster behind Sephora. Dive in. Swim around until the creams and serums penetrate your skull.

Back at home, take the syringes of "Botox" that you bought on the Darknet out of the freezer.

Follow the misspelled instructions as best you can, considering your eyelids are rigidly trying to snap shut behind your eyeballs. That means it's working!

Light your whole goddamned head on fire. Fuck you. Fuck. You.

Grandma Lidia's in hell now.

Unspool one of the ancient scrolls you found in that box by the lake. Read the words. How can you read these words?

Once the demons are gone, pack your face in gauze. Wait four clicks of a scorpion's pincer. Remove the gauze.

Stare at the unholy goddess before you. No one can ever know what happened here.

Splash your face with cold water!

THESE MALE POP STARS THINK YOU'RE BEAUTIFUL AND YOU DON'T EVEN KNOW IT

If you don't know you're beautiful yet, here are some things that our favorite male feminists and/or pop musicians have said about you.

Bruno Mars

"You're amazing just the way you are. . . . You're not wearing makeup, are you? Oh, you are? Well then, make sure you always have it on, because that's apparently how you are when I love you."

Adam Levine

"Look for the girl with the broken smile. Ask her if she wants to fuck awhile. Every woman is fuckable, even the ones with jacked-up teeth. I'm Adam Levine."

One Direction (except Zayn)

"You don't know you're beautiful, even though I keep telling you, girl. Are you stupid?"

FEELING BEAUTIFUL IS THE NEW LOOKING BEAUTIFUL

These days, looking beautiful is no longer enough—now we have to *feel* beautiful too. There is a growing awareness for this need for a greater feeling of beautifulness in women. Fortunately, many brands are pitching in to lift up our down-at-the-heels inner beauty in addition to our looks. For instance, more and more corporations are noticing precisely when and why we don't like ourselves and are finally starting to help us fix it.

But buying these awesome products that benefit your sense of inner beauty isn't the only thing you can do to make yourself feel beautiful. It's time to totally revitalize your inner image, with this how-to on giving yourself *a makeover for your self-esteem!*

This make-*om*-ver will totally transform the way you look and feel *underneath your skin.* While looking great on the outside can impact how you feel inside, having a strong sense of self-worth on the inside can impact how you feel on the outside, which will affect how you look on the outside, which will make you feel good on the inside. Get it? Here's how to do it.

Find a mantra that flatters the contours of your self-worth.

Every girl worth her Oprah's book-club membership knows that affirmations are the perfect tools for improving your confidence and self-image. Find one you can get behind, one that really hugs the curves of your current ego, flaws and all. You want to camouflage problem areas in your self-esteem without totally hiding your inner self in oversize, baggy perceptions.

Try a mantra with a flattering silhouette that nips in at your narrow-waisted conceptions of yourself—something like "I *did* walk a lot today, actually." Wear dark-wash jeans and control-top thoughts to downplay your larger areas in self-perception with an affirmation like, "No one really looks at legs, anyway. Faces are so much more engaging!" We knew your inner self had a waist in there, somewhere!

Lop off those weighty negative self-perceptions.

Over the years, many women's self-image gets weighed down by long, heavy, tired old tresses of self-abuse. You'll want to trim those to discover a new shorter, more youthful self-image that better frames your inner face. So stop hiding behind thoughts like, "I need to get to the gym," and instead think, "A cleanse could be sort of fun, actually." Cutting off all those metaphorical dead ends of thought will have people thinking your inner self doesn't look a day over thirty. While you're at it, get some inner highlights! Your guy won't even recognize you (on the inside)!

Figure out your inner bra size.

Take your *internal* measurements. Eighty-five percent of women are wearing a wrong-size self-image. Your self-perception requires support; otherwise the physical you will hang badly on the inner you. You want a big, perky feeling of beautifulness for an inner figure that shows through all the layers of your persona. You'll also want your inner bra to lift and separate your inner boobs.

Don't be afraid of color (in your emotional wardrobe).

So many women go around with the same old "I'm okay" black-and-white thinking. But allowing yourself to wear a variety of emotional states will help you highlight your most vibrant, glowing inner self. Brighten up a Monday with a zany yellow emotion, where you get crazy and e-mail coworkers a bunch of nonsensical "ideas" to "jazz up the office." On a Friday night with your guy, try on a fiery red anger and accuse him of cheating. Remembering to reignite these seldom-used emotional colors will reaffirm that your inner self is still alive and young and beautiful.

Take off your inner glasses.

Women often get too focused on doing "inner work" to better themselves emotionally. But sometimes you need to stop riding your self-esteem so hard, take off those inner glasses, let your hair down, have a glass of wine, and *relax* (on the inside). It can be so sexy when your inner self lets go.

Throw on some inner heels.

Is your inner self slouching, hunched over? A pair of inner heels can do wonders to make your self-perception stand tall, lengthening legs and puffing out that chest—you don't want that new inner bra to go to waste, do you? It's a good idea to find a comfortable and versatile pair of heels for your staple inner wardrobe that you can pair with any inner look for whatever function your inner self and you have to attend. Black pumps are a must-own!

WE SWEAR
OUR PLEDGE
$1 from every copy of this book sold will go toward making women *feel* beautiful.

Lose weight!

This tip's actually for your outer self, but it will definitely make your inner self look and feel better. You're worth it, inside and out!

It may seem like a lot now, but with a few key changes to the way you dress up your inner self, you'll be *feeling* beautiful in no time. Remember, inner blondes have all the fun!

FEMINIST COSMETIC TOOLS

Nothing gets you feeling feminist in the morning or before a night out like a powerful, unique look. Feminists favor bold looks that aren't afraid to make people take notice. We're not invisible, and neither is our makeup! Think power brows, strong cheekbones, a contoured cheek *and* hairstyle. But getting there takes a little work—work that only a strong feminist has the power to undertake. Feministify your routine with these feminist cosmetic tools!

SexyBabyGurl 3-in-1 Brow Shaper

While this device may look like something out of a horror movie, it's actually the perfect tool to get you looking like the femme fatale out of a horror movie. Unlike overprocessed girly girls, feminists prefer a simpler, chic brow look. So add this shaper to your tweezing routine, before smoothing those brows with your brow brush and setting them with an eyebrow gel. The only thing stronger than your feminist outlook is how stubbornly those brow hairs root themselves into your skin! So tame those unruly brows to show people what an unbending will you have when it comes to fighting the patriarchy! Get those feminist eyebrows to frame that feminist perspective!

Drunk Diva Exfoliating Face Scraper

Got that exhausted dead face that comes from listening to the patriarchy yammer on and on about your uterus? Well, wipe that man-tiredness off your lifeless face, so you can feminist another day—with Drunk Diva's Exfoliating Face Scraper. The people at Drunk Diva want the real you to shine through!

Tit-Factory Acidahyde Express Face Serum Resin

Are your ears burning? We hope so! And also your face and neck when you apply this liberally all over your skull skin as directed on the packaging. People will be talking about how radiant you look and wondering what that "interesting" smell is. It's the tiny acid beads burning off the top (and in our opinion completely useless) layer of your epidermis. Now there's the fresh-faced girl whose voice men don't find grating! Get ready to have your feminist thoughts heard! And unlike Tit-Factory's first-generation Acidahyde Face Serum, this one is FDA-approved to leave on all day, working hard underneath your makeup, while you work hard at gender equality!

Yum! Facefood Sticky-Candy Face-Torture Lip-Wax Kit

Waxing your lip can be so painful, especially if there's hair there! But this lip-waxing kit by Yum! Facefood uses a patented formula that smells and tastes like honey (even if the manufacturer doesn't recommend you ingest it!). The rip action you can get off of just one strip will have your mustache hairs *and* oppressive patriarchal structures shaking in their boots!

Abadadubadawamapa Night Nose Cream

Dry flaky morning nose got you all tensed up before your big-strong-woman day? Having a hard time envisioning having it all, when you don't even have a hydrated nose? The creators of Abadadubadawamapa came up with the idea for this nose cream and its name when they got drunk-lost on a yoga retreat and started chanting themselves to sleep. "To me it feels like it means love," says CEO Dani Zickerson. "Love and strength and moisture and women. That's what we're all about. Also wine, duh!"

Your conscience will love it too, since the proceeds go to women in the third world! The products are made by barely wealthy American women* living simple lives in the planet's most beautiful English-speaking third-world countries, teaching yoga to all who will listen. What better way to start your feminist day than by supporting a company that supports women *and* supports your face?!

Lady Shark Collagenelastinin Supplements

Lady Shark Collagenelastinin supplements take the most rubbery part of the shark (shark butt) and put it to good use by providing you with the nutrients to have a strong face. Pop these pills five times a day, and your face will have the strength and elasticity to say, "No, I will *not* smile for you, stranger, even though I have a really, really great smile." Finally women will have the opportunities that sharks have had all along, with smiles that scare people.

---

* Who left their corporate jobs to find something "more authentic."

Remember, being feminist doesn't mean being ugly. It just means being a stronger, more empowered kind of pretty. So check out these face-improvement tools to put on your best feminist face!

HOW TO LOVE YOUR BODY EVEN THOUGH HERS IS BETTER

With all of the messages out there telling you that your body isn't good enough, it's hard to tune out the negativity and love your body just the way it is—especially because your friend Jen's body is objectively better than your body, which is just kind of okay looking.

But the world is filled with all kinds of beautiful bodies—that's what makes the world so interesting! Your body is part of the rich tapestry that makes up humanity, which is really just a collection of bodies woven together as a society. It's important to remember that you're just as much a part of that, even if you're not quite as flawless a part of it as Jen is with her smoking abs and perfect limbs. After all, life isn't about achieving perfection, unless you're Jen, in which case it seems to happen pretty naturally.

Here are some ways to refocus your energy and love your body, even though hers is definitely better.

Your body is a temple, but some temples are holier than other temples.

You've heard the old adage, "Your body is a temple," and you owe it to yourself to treat it like one. But even in ancient times, some temples were popular with tourists while others crumbled away in the woods, so it's valuable to assess where your temple stands in relation to other, more conventionally attractive, awe-inspiring temples. Once you realize that your body is at best a second-rate temple with some blatant structural flaws, you can learn to love it for what it is and worship at it accordingly. Jen's even-toned, proportional temple just happens to be the Angkor Wat of bodies—but your body really is holy and sacred too!

Walk with your head held high, even though Jen's got a solid five inches on you.

Sometimes the world can beat us down and make us slump our shoulders and hang our heads. But our physical stature affects how we feel on the inside as well. Puff your chest out and keep your head held high, and you'll notice an immediate boost in how you feel about yourself. Until you run into Jen, who is a solid five inches taller than you and really *owns* it, you know?

Wear clothes that feel good on your body, because Jen's clothes would be too tight and unflattering on you.

So many of us have spent years trying to fit into clothes and styles that make us feel inadequate, especially if we ever went shopping with Jen or believed her when she encouraged us to borrow things from her closet "because we're basically the same size." Try something that fits *your* body that makes *you* feel comfortable instead. Try some flowing linen pants and a loose-fitting top, something that isn't constantly reminding you to suck it in or not run too fast in fear of ripping your pants. Remind yourself that constant discomfort will never make anybody happy—Jen knows that. Skinny jeans just really "work" for her.

Keep a note on your mirror that says, "I accept what I see even though I see a lot of things that are better."

Keeping a positive mantra stuck to your mirror will help change the way you perceive yourself over time. Whenever you look in the mirror, say, "I accept what I see," knowing full well that there are a lot of things out there that are much better.* Realistically, if there's one Jen out there, there are probably thousands of perfect Jens of all different races all over the world, and there's nothing you can do about it. Remember, this is about acceptance!!

Happiness is not a body shape. It's accepting where you are in relation to Jen.

No matter what lengths you go through to change your body, there is no "perfect" body shape that will bring you happiness. You have to find it within yourself and in relation to Jen. Everybody deserves happiness; some people just get more than others! Be true to yourself, and you'll find out exactly how much happiness you deserve compared to Jen.

And there you have it. You're a beautiful, special person who deserves love and acceptance. And just so you know, Jen is already way ahead of you on that. You might want to join her at her meditation class and see how it goes.

---

* Jen.

SIX PHOTOS TO HELP YOU LOVE YOUR BODY MORE

Jen blinking.

Jen sleeping in a gross way.

Jen during her awkward tween years.

Jen working out.

A picture of you and Jen with Jen cropped out.

This tiny bug!

Real Women Have Lumps . . . Gym!

Real women are strong, beautiful, and not afraid to show off their Lumps Gym membership.

Here at Lumps Gym, we love your lumps. Lumps are sexy! But some women believe that their lumps aren't good enough. We want you to *celebrate your lumps* by sort of getting rid of them a little. But not too much! You are beautiful just the way you are. *But now is the time for change.*

Real women have Lumps.

Fitness isn't just about fitting into a size 0, or starving yourself, or breaking both of your legs in a horrific exercise accident; it's about *feeling good in your own body.* Your lumps are a symbol of your womanhood; you've got to celebrate them! Honor them through exercise that will liberate them from your body. You're beautiful!

It's a gym! For women!

We're not here to make you lose weight. We're here to *transform your life* in a process that will result in your losing weight. After all, it's not about changing your body; it's about *changing your whole self* by changing your body. In a way that *only women can do.* #Lumpsstrong

Women, it's time to come together! Empower yourself and your friends through group workouts, storytelling in a circle, stretching on a tumbling mat, and more.

Here at Lumps, every woman is the same, but also uniquely different.

That's why we give you your Lumps SisterName that your sisters can call you within the sacred Lumps walls. We are here to foster solidarity among women, but also to highlight your unique differences, and also to have you do exercises in order to lose weight. But not a crazy amount of weight! That's not what the Lumps philosophy is about. Unless that's part of your personal journey. In which case, we support you!

TRY OUR NEW 11-MINUTE CLASSES!

New Class! No-Impact Warrior Boxing

Like the toughness of boxing without all of the hitting? Strap on your gloves and get ready for our seven-minute, no-impact, boxing-inspired movement class, where a certified boxing trainer guides you through a series of yoga poses meant to inspire the warrior inside. Afterward, we'll spend twenty minutes lying down and breathing. Women need to let themselves breathe!

For Mall Walkers: Lumps Mall!

This mall was made for walkin'! Our signature Lumps Mall is great for mall walkers who need a safe space to get walking with other like-minded, strong women. With stairs, long hallways, ramps, and plenty of water fountains, our mall was custom designed to fit your fitness goals. Also, it's a mall!

New! The Orange Is the New Black Workout!

We're excited to announce our inaugural *Orange Is the New Black* workout! We'll put you in our own simulation of a women's prison, which is a room in the back of every participating Lumps gym.* You'll get to interact with all kinds of hilarious characters and other *real women, just like you,* and move your body the way women's bodies were meant to be moved—with arms crossed, glaring across the room at your assigned partner/lesbian lover. (Fact: Lesbian trysts can help you burn an extra 100 calories during your workout.)

Lumps Gym features a uniquely designed-for-her experience that includes:

- Naps
- On-site Therapists
- Holding Hands
- A Ball Pit!

- Frozen Lumps Meals
- Hugs!
- Arts and Crafts
- *Vagina Monologues*

- Business Management and Starting Your Own Lumps Franchise

From Our Success Stories:

"*I lost over 98 pounds at Lumps. I learned to love my body by changing it altogether. I also learned to love my former lumpy self while becoming the less lumpy me I am today. Lumps Gym is the BEST!!!*"—Kristy L., Iowa

"*I spent most of my adult life power-walking through malls. But ever since I found Lumps, I've been walking in their own Lumps Mall, designed just for women! I'm still exactly the same, but now I love myself.*"—Lauren P., Oklahoma

"*I actually gained 11 pounds at Lumps Gym, but I did make a ton of friends! Also, that mall has great sales!*"—Candy G., New York

—SPONSORED BY THE ALLIANCE FOR WOMEN IN FITNESS BUSINESS AND GYMS—

---

* It also includes the showers.

JUST THE RIGHT AMOUNT OF SEXINESS!

If *Sex and the City* taught us one thing,* it's that it's totally cool to be sex positive—everybody wants to be Carrie—but the Miranda or Samantha of the group will still get some eye rolls. Finding the right amount of sexiness takes careful styling. You want a look that says, "I'm sexy and a little edgy, but I work in an office." And while stiletto heels may have been empowering for fictional sex columnists in the early aughts, they just won't cut it for a girl trying to get a promotion at her hedge fund in 2020. Like other modern feminists, you prefer a more downplayed look, one that's soft but strong and playful in a nonthreatening way!

The Hair

Tousled: Not Feminist

Messy hair gives men the idea that you're just rolling from bed to bed, that you're weak and ready to be taken advantage of. You want to give the impression that you're pro-choice, but not because you personally have had a bunch of abortions.

Bun: Not Feminist

Buns are universally scary and almost never sexy (unless they're on a bride, in which case she's playing up that "Yeah right, like *I'm* a virgin" jokey vibe). Buns may have had a certain sexy edge for first-wave 1840s feminists, but these days they are just not pushing enough buttons politically or sexually. Unless you're a child ballet prodigy, and even then it's first-wave, like, baby-hot, which is kind of gross.

Half-Shaved Head with Long Waves: Feminist as Fuck!

This powerful but sweet look tells people, "I love women. I've even fooled around with one or two. Respect our rights (but hey, I'm not gonna burn down your fraternity or anything)." The half-shaved head with waves gives off a fierce but ultimately happy hippie vibe.

The Outfit

Strappy Dress: Not Feminist

Yikes! A flirty little dress is *so* last decade and basically tells men to walk all over you. It says, "I'm doing all the listening at this cocktail party and none of the talking."

---

* *Sex and the City* taught us a lot of things.

Blazer: Not Feminist

A blazer creates a harsh silhouette that emasculates men and threatens other women. Women who wear blazers make other people fear that they'll never stop interrupting and talking over them, even if they haven't said anything at all. If you're going to wear a blazer, you may as well hold a big fucking knife in your hand.

Blazer with Bodycon Dress: Oh, Fuck Yeah!

This look is feminine, but strong, letting people know you're good at sex *and* business. You're not afraid to take part in the conversation, with flirty quips like, "Ha ha ha, that's funny, Mark! You killed in that presentation. Wanna get out of here?"

The Nails

Long Red Nails: Not Feminist

Long, fire-engine-red nails are like a blaring siren that tells men your body is open for sex. Your nails may as well be airport marshals waving him toward the runway of your vagina. This look could not be more blatant or crude about how undiscriminating you are toward the penis planes you clear for landing.

No Polish: Not Feminist

When women step out with unvarnished tips, they come off as depressed or potentially violent. Don't be caught dead with dry, naked nails. Polish-free nails are like a vast expanse of desert, with a sign warning men, "Turn back, lest ye perish here." Don't let those nails go bare unless you want to send out an "I punch every dick I see" vibe.

Red Nail Polish on Short Nails: Feminist Bomb DROPPED

Red nail polish on short, neatly buffed nails lets people know you're sexually active but also physically, professionally, and politically active. You're not a high-maintenance long-nail girl, but you're also not a cursed corpse in a coffin. You're a fun, soft, fun, strong (but not rip-off-your-nuts strong), fun feminist.

Finding just the right amount of sexiness to suit your new feminist perspective can be tough. Luckily if you follow these rules, you'll forever separate yourself from the "basic" and "too much" wrong-amount-of-sex-having antifeminists out there. *Get it, girl!*

---

* Within reason.

WHICH NONFEMINIST CLOTHES ARE IN YOUR CLOSET *RIGHT NOW*?

As modern-day feminists, we know that clothes are a great way to play up our feminine strength, but there are a lot of woman-harming clothes out there that women don't even know about. These problematic clothes hold us back from being on an even playing field with men. *Especially* in your intramural bocce ball league. You would have won last year's title if Asha hadn't worn clogs!!

Beware! These misogynist garments might even be in your ameeeezing reclaimed barn-wood wardrobe right now. You can feel their day-ruining energy. They're clothes that keep us from looking our best. Clothes that keep us from being perceived as strong and fierce. Clothes that keep us from being *us*. Simply put: *us deserve better*.

It's not enough to toss these types of clothing that are *actively harming* you as a woman. You must also help prevent other women from falling victim to these damaging* fashions. Here are the clothes you should be vocally, actively *against*. Here are the clothes to protest.

Capris

Would a man wear capris? Not if he was running his own company, that's for sure.** Capris and clamdiggers make us look ridiculous, giving the impression that women should be relegated to the dunes. Don't wear them unless you want to set yourself and womankind back half a decade. If a salesperson tries to sell you on capris, say, "What do I look like, a clam shucker? Would you ask me to wear a big vagina*** on my shirt?!" Sorry lady, my body, my calf-length choice.

EXCEPTIONS: Black high-waist capris with flats. Chic! *#Audrey*

HOW TO PROTEST: Create a Tumblr where you Photoshop full-length pants onto any images you can find of women wearing capris. Trust us, they'll thank you, and you'll grow the public's awareness of the "shortcomings" of these horrible "pants." We have a social responsibility to enact change! Our pants are our future!

INSTEAD WEAR: Skirts! Throw on something freeing and body-conscious, like a short skirt. Just don't wear a skirt with pockets. Pockets imply you'll be carrying things around for men—nice try, men!

---

* This word gives us all the feels!

** Notable exceptions: Dutch billionaires on vacation, marijuantrepreneurs, I-bankers with very long legs.

*** Actually, this would be kind of cool and definitely feminist.

FEMINISTS WE ADMIRE: ELLIE MUNSON, FOUNDER OF CRITICAL CAPRI

Ellie Munson was tired of seeing women be victimized by offensive and demeaning looks, such as capris, so she founded Critical Capri. Every week, Critical Capri gathers at offending stores such as Old Navy and Lane Bryant, clogging up the walkways and shopping lanes, holding full-length pants above their heads. "We're attempting to disrupt capri wearage in the most effective way we've found," says Munson. "Women are stronger and better than this and shouldn't be made to feel like capris are an okay way to be treated by the clothing industry." Wow! We salute you, Ellie!

Wedges

Where are you going in these? Are you getting paid? We think not, unless that barbecue is paying you a day rate. Your mouth is saying "I'd like a raise," but your shoes are screaming "Bridal shower!!!" Do you want to be an entrepreneur or just the girl who sneaks wine into an outdoor Mozart concert? Wedges are the embodiment of half-confidence in footwear. The wearer is committing to neither a work nor play time of day. These shoes transition you from "Who am I?" to "What?" Know yourself. Know your power. And don't wear these power-sapping shoes.

EXCEPTIONS: Black patent wedges. Get it!

HOW TO PROTEST: Use the hashtag #yesallwedges on social media when posting about the horrors of wedges. *Example:* "Cork belongs in my wine, not in my shoes! Who's coming to this concert??? #Mozart #yesallwedges." Hashtag activism is a great way for like-minded individuals to support each other's perspectives on wedges.

INSTEAD WEAR: High heels! Nothing says powerful feminist like a sexy pair of heels.

Bandana Tops

Real women deserve real shirts, or at least a cute bralette under a blazer. A bandana top says, "I'll just tie these boobs down in a shirt that points down at my vagina like it's a problem to be fixed to indicate that I'm ashamed of my own body." Real change starts at the top, so start empowering yourself by wearing the tops you deserve. There's a reason men don't wear bandana tops, and the reason is self-respect.

EXCEPTIONS: Black leather bandana tops with black bikini bottoms. Hot!

HOW TO PROTEST: Get a group of friends together to burn bandana tops.

INSTEAD WEAR: Nothing at all. Real feminists aren't afraid to be sexy!

MENSES: THE ORIGINAL FEMINIST ACCESSORY

In the beginning, women made babies, and it was thought to be dark magic, brought forth from the blood that fell from them each month. Early priests called it the "crimson curse." But one day, in ancient Egypt, the first brave woman took a look at her stained undergarments and said, "You know what? We can work with this." And her gay Egyptian friend, who was not unlike Tim Gunn, said, "Yes, make it work." She then wiped that blood on her face, and the original feminist accessory came into being.

Doing away with outdated feminine hygiene standards, and replacing them with cooler ones!

Even today, nothing threatens the power of men like showcasing our reproductive powers out in the open, front and center, forcing them to look our creative force dead in the eye. The modern woman is no longer afraid to flaunt her bloody femininity, because a good feminist is proud of her body, no matter *what* it does. And now, through our support and these recently resurrected ancient stone slabs, she can wear her period on her sleeve with pride. Here are some slick ways to accessorize with girl blood as preserved in Egyptian hieroglyphs!

Here's a rough translation by Britt-Britt, our resident Egyptologist and social-media manager:

SLAVES, TRY THIS 3-IN-1 FACE STAIN!

Hey, girl, did Min—the god of fertility, reproduction, and lettuce—fail in blessing you with a baby this month and leave only lettuce? Ugh, been there! You might be bleedin' out that puss-puss, but that doesn't mean it's a total loss. Yesterday's no-baby shame is today's beauty stain! Check it out: your menses is the perfect all-natural stain for the eyes, lips, and cheeks! Here's how to get the look:

- Following the line of your cheekbone, apply a thin layer of menses evenly and blend into your locust-ravaged skin.

- Line and fill your parched lips with menses. Maybe even drink some! God damn, when is that pyramid gonna be done?!

- Fill the crease of your eye with a dramatic dollop of menses to get the sexy cat-eye effect. Bastet-approved!

Your face is glowing, like that amulet you should never have touched. The gods will bless you with your husband's penis—if he ever finishes that darn pyramid! Soon there'll be a baby. Now, get back to work before he sees your woman tricks.

Wow! Those ancient Egyptian slave chicks were prescient. Could they ever have imagined what they were setting in motion for modern women embracing their beauty?

Note: For health reasons we do not recommend putting actual blood on your face. Use this as inspiration for applying real makeup.

DESIGNER HANDBAGS TO HOLD ALL YOUR FEMINISM

Walking the feminist walk and talking the feminist talk are hard work. In between trips to Neiman Marcus, barre class, and your personal vajazzler, it takes a lot of tricks and tools to keep up your feminist values. You'll need a bag that can survive the wear and tear of slogging through the day, while holding everything you need—lipsticks to suit the changing light of the day (available at Neiman Marcus), this book, a healthy snack, and a warm sweater for your office's air-conditioning (available at Neiman Marcus).

Julie Lurch Mademoiselle Backpack in Lip ($9,293)

Ughhhh, we would rather die than not have this backpack in our handbag storage locker. It is like the candy of bags. Too sweet to touch, but too colorful to look away from! The *genius* designer Julie Lurch put a diamond inside on the label. A real fucking *diamond*. Empowerment. Pack it up with mothballs, because you are going to live forever.

Rumer Willis Small Lady Bowler in One Tone ($768)

We nearly fainted in our flats when we heard that our fave Willis girl started designing handbags. Thank our bald father-God she got in the game, 'cause this little bowler is holding everything we need—from our teeth-bleaching lozenges to our midday foot scrub! Being a woman is fun again!

Compte de LaDumpte Hello? Am I Alive? Shrunken Suitcase in Swine Rose ($2,873)

The sleek lines and minimalist hardware of this—whaaatever—you just *need* this to assert your womanhood. So good. Put all things in it.

Humbleberry Tubbleburns Froppled Leather Smatchel in Vole Mouth ($5,494)

Ow, my eyes! Put this on my arm, or I'll fall into a coma! I don't care if there's a nine-month waiting list, and you can only get on it if you're the shopgirl's aunt! Mummy wants! Mummy get this for me!

Feminists are just like other women, but more enlightened. And like other women, they need very nice handbags, available at a Neiman Marcus near you, to feel whole.

PERFECTING THE NO-SELF SELFIE

You've already got the no-makeup selfie down pat,* so what's the next step? How can you step up your minimalist self-portrait game, you understated-face-serving trailblazer you?

Your Instagram followers rely on you to blow their minds with humble, natural-seeming shots, so it might be time for you to go with the nuclear option: *the no-self selfie*. By removing your ego-soaked physical form and just showing people the stark reality of your surroundings, you're showing them the real you—the invisible you who is reflected in the things she looks at or sits near.

"But wait," you're thinking. "How does it qualify as a selfie if I'm not in it?"

Trust us, girl. We know how scary it is to be totally raw. The Internet is *not* the most forgiving place to be a woman who's willing to be *real*. But it'll be worth the risk once you see how well people respond to your real rawness.**

Bottom line: it takes a strong woman to show others the room she's in, naked of herself.

Here's how to get the look.

1. Hire a professional makeup artist.

Just because your face isn't in frame doesn't mean you can look like an uggo corpse. The room will absorb the vibes it gets from you. What kind of vibes do you want to put out? That's right—pretty vibes. Remember, the universe reflects what it sees in us, even if the universe in this instance is just your bathroom walls. Let them see the "you" you want to be by contracting the services of an excellent makeup artist who has experience in fashion and editorial beauty looks.*** What's a few hundred dollars when you're feeling beautiful *and* humble?

---

* Full blowout + too much bright light + lots and lots of makeup (but like, tasteful).

** Raw realness?

*** We tried this with and without makeup, and blind test groups preferred the with-makeup no-self selfie, hands down.

2. Get a blowout.

Giving your locks the love they deserve is a must for the no-self selfie. Big voluminous hair will help diffuse any light coming from behind you as you stand *behind* the camera, giving your photo a soft halolike glow. Also, you should be getting blowouts if you want to look presentable anyway. Make an appointment at whichever blow-dry-only salon is the most expensive in your area. You're worth it! There's nothing aspirational about being a bargain hunter.

3. Avoid processed foods.

The idea is for the picture to not have you in it. This will be easier to accomplish if your body takes up less space. Before you get upset, think about it. Big things are big. Make sense? Make your body small by eschewing anything with a label and eat a diet comprised primarily of whole foods like leaves, lettuces, plants, and leaves. This will help your you-less picture look its best!*

4. Set the scene.

The environment you choose for your no-self selfie is just as important as how you look off-camera. Make sure your house is huge and beautiful before you start taking pictures of it. No one wants to look at a sad little prefab rental, so take out some loans and buy the house of your wildest, craziest, least-sane dreams. If you can't have a big pretty house, ask your richest friend** if you can borrow hers. Put as many of your most adorably twee and expensive items in the shot as possible. Toss a throw from Anthro over the back of your Eames sofa and arrange your favorite Jonathan Adler objets d'art on your reclaimed redwood coffee table. Gorgeous!

If for some reason you can't*** find a good indoor location, a gorgeous beach or valley will do. Just choose the most private-looking, "I think I saw Leo DiCaprio here once—this could be Europe" spot, so no one thinks you're broke.

---

* And least you.

** Hint: she's the one who always looks clean and doesn't sweat, like, at all.

*** Won't?

5. Position your lighting rig.

Most of photography is about getting the right light, so cut no corners when it comes to setting up your lighting equipment. Oh, you're not used to using cinematic lighting elements to take a simple snapshot? Well, then, our mistake. Toss this book in the trash and go back to snorting Pixy Stix, or whatever it is you were doing. For everyone else, if you need to rent lighting pieces you don't own, like a crane, so be it. This is *your time*.

6. Frame it up.

Decide where exactly you'll point the camera to maximize the impact of your no-self selfie. Make sure to include your purest essence in the composition of the shot. You want to show people just how ethereal you really are—you can disappear into thin air!* Most important, avoid reflective surfaces like mirrors, stainless-steel sculptures, and shiny marble walls. You don't want to actually be in it; you want to *spiritually* be in it. Does your head hurt yet? Ours too! Beauty is pain. Keep going!

7. Snap!

Ready, aim, fired! The amount of time you've spent on your online presence may have gotten you canned from your job, but that's something you can think about later. For now, all you need to do is hit that button a few thousand times. The siren call of this selfie trend demands an answer!!

8. Filter, filter, filter.

Once you comb through all the footage, select the humanless shot that makes you look the most inspirational.** Then upload the picture of your rich boyfriend's breakfast nook to a photo-editing app.*** Throw on whatever filter best brings out your brand: low contrast, high saturation, sepia tone, or even anime-inspired sparkles. Filters help us hide the bad, emphasize the good, and totally fabricate a perfect, beautiful, egoless lie. And that's beautiful!

---

* Emphasis on thin!

** A.k.a. "fuckable."

*** If you're still using Instagram's prefab filters, we have literally nothing to offer you.

9. Caption it.

Choose from the following list:

Just be.	Be just being.
Just breathe.	Humbles.
Breathe.	Be blessed.
Humbled.	"Keep calm and carry on." —Ram Dass
Blessed.	Humbly bumbly.
"Be the change you wish to see in the world." —Mahatma Gandhi	"You may say that I'm a dreamer, but I'm not the only one." —Marilyn Monroe
Be. The.	Humbled.
Be breath.	Breath blessed.
Just.	

10. Hashtag it.

Pick your poison! And remember, there's no such thing as too many hashtags.

#namaste	#oatmeal*
#inspired	#breathe
#yogi	#beauty
#literallyselfless	#house
#aintnome	#ramdass
#glutenfreehealthgirl	#eatcleanmovenourishbelievestarttoday
#fitspo	#meditation
#fitlifeclearheartcantlose	

And there you have it: the perfect no-self selfie! Make sure to post mid-afternoon, when everyone's low on blood sugar and feeling dreamy. You look ameezing!! Get it, girl!!!

---

* Don't worry if there's no oatmeal in the shot. Your main audience is people who love looking at oatmeal on Instagram.

WHY ALL WOMEN DESERVE EQUAL ACCESS TO PHOTOSHOP

When Photoshop is not easily accessible, women suffer.
Women without access to safe and reliable photo-editing tools have been forced by circumstance to share busted selfies that affect their quality of life for years to come. Is this what we want? Is this *America*?

It's up to us to give all women increased access to life-saving Photoshop tools. *Every* woman deserves to be Photoshopped in a way that reflects her power, intelligence, and the flawless complexion that she doesn't actually have but theoretically *could*.

Far too many women are being left behind in the workforce because their LinkedIn profile pic makes them look bloated, tired, old, sad, or just kind of how they look on a normal day—the equivalent of showing up to work minus a full face of makeup.

Sure, we could try to fix the problem at the root and erase the systems that perpetuate this problem that is specific to women, but looking good isn't just fun—it's *vital*. Our solution? Share that vital fun by raising money to give women across the country equal access to Photoshop.

Here are some crucial statistics about the impact of Photoshop on women's lives.

Did you know that women without access to Photoshop have 51 percent fewer Tinder matches?
It's true. For every Tinder match that you receive, women without access to Photoshop receive less than half that number—that's not even a whole person! How are you going to date or hook up with 49 percent of a person? You can't. No woman deserves to be left behind on Tinder.

Did you know that 98 percent of women living in war-torn nations do not have access to Photoshop?
The numbers are staggering. Women living in war zones are significantly more at risk for being without Photoshop or a similar photo-editing tool, or a computer, or even a friend with Instagram on her phone. In many countries, women are forced to scrape the printed images of themselves with crude bayonets to remove blemishes and erase wrinkles. That is *no* healing brush. Most women don't even get one solid bathroom-mirror selfie before thirty. Hard to hear, but it's true.

Did you know that every female CEO has had access to Photoshop in her lifetime?
You already knew that women struggled to get a leg up in the workforce—try being a CEO who's a 6 on a good day. No woman has reached the top of the corporate food chain without safe, abundant access to the various kinds of blurring available in Photoshop. How are you going to be a corporate leader without the most fundamental tools of manipulation?

Did you know that the children of women without Photoshop are less likely to love their moms? Can you even blame them?
You want your daughter to think you're beautiful on the inside *and* out, don't you? Do you want to be a worthy role model for her? A role model worthy of her love? How are you going to do that without Photoshop?

All women were born equally flawed and deserve equal opportunity to present themselves exactly how they want to be presented. We believe all women are beautiful on the inside, and we're fighting to ensure that all women receive equal access to Photoshop. If you are committed to helping other women, join the fight and donate your pirated copy to a woman in need. You *do* care about other women, right?

Right?

PAID FOR BY THE NATIONAL SOCIETY FOR THE ADVANCEMENT OF WOMEN'S APPEARANCE (NSAWA)

EMBRACING DIFFERENCES: TEACHING MODELS WHAT IT WOULD BE LIKE TO BE FAT

It can be easy to look at models and think, "They have no idea what it's like for us *real* women." But we wanted to give models the benefit of the doubt and see if they had what it takes to open their eyes to the experiences of other-bodied and differently jiggled people. So we took these four size 0 models and had them try on size 10 (plus-size) clothing in an attempt to replicate the experiences of what *real* women feel in the fitting room, when the clothes available just don't fit. You won't believe the results!

"This is kind of cute actually. I could cinch it with a belt."—Genesis, twenty-three
Body positivity! Genesis gets that you can have a hard time finding clothes that fit you and still love the way you look!

"Oh my God, is this how big the average woman is?!
I look so tiny. I love it! I'm wearing this tonight."—Kalatrina, twenty-two
Oops. That's not what we were going for. But cool!

"Can I keep this?"—Jordayné, twenty-three
I mean, we can't say she doesn't have great taste! We did put a lot of effort into this, and we appreciate the enthusiasm!

"Have you guys thought of selling this for real?
This shit is dope."—Kahleesi, eighteen
They actually *do* sell these clothes! Imagine . . .

We were stunned at how successful this experiment was. Although we started with the intention of teaching these models what it was like to wonder if something was wrong with *her* rather than the clothes, each of these girls walked out of our studio with something really slouchy and cute that she can wear dressed up or down. Powerful.

OUR INSPIRATION: DIVERSE WOMEN IN MEDIA

When it comes to film and television, there's nothing more important than film and television. And when it comes to finding models for our feminist selves in other strong, beautiful women, there's no better place to look to than Tinseltown! But we don't want to emulate the white-bread, cookie-cutter actresses who used to grace the stage and screen. We want to take inspiration from the diverse, fresh faces of *right now*.

Some media critics decry a serious lack of diversity in Hollywood. Despite many intrinsic biases in the entertainment industry, a few megatalented megastar megatalents from unique backgrounds have managed to have megacareers, proving once and for all that there is room for diversity in the media! Given the weight we place on these stars, equal representation is hugely important and should be at the forefront of entertainment executives' minds. Let's applaud and celebrate Hollywood's diversity with a list of some of the most ethnic and diverse celebrities in Hollywood today.

SCARLETT JOHANSSON: You might be thinking, "Who, *her?*" That's right! This luscious-lipped A-lister is half Jewish. Put *her* in more movies!!

LINDSAY LOHAN: As America's sweetheart turned bad girl, Lindsay Lohan is no stranger to living life in the public eye. But something that may have escaped that gaze is her hidden ethnic background: Lohan is half Italian. Wow! What are the odds?!

HAYDEN PANETTIERE: Known for her star turns on *Heroes* and *Nashville,* this country cutie is part German. *Guten Tag!* So brave.

ROONEY MARA: The girl from *The Girl with the Dragon Tattoo* has porcelain skin and dark hair. You might not know it, but her Canadian ancestors had French surnames, suggesting that they were of French Canadian descent! It's so good to see diversity on screen.

AMY ADAMS: This Academy Award–nominated actress is known for her gorgeous red hair and pale, pale skin. You'd never know that she was actually born in Italy! How's *that* for diversity?

EMMA STONE: Miss Stone found herself embroiled in a racial controversy over her portrayal of a quarter Chinese, quarter Hawaiian character in Cameron Crowe's 2015 film *Aloha.* Maybe those activists would have thought twice about protesting if they knew she was one-eighth Pennsylvania Dutch!

BETTY WHITE: Don't be fooled by her last name! Although this golden girl may *look* 100 percent WASP, she's also part Danish. Who knew?

DIANNA AGRON: The *Glee* starlet was raised in a Jewish home and once e-mailed with a German person. Wow! Diversity double whammy!

DAKOTA FANNING: After wowing audiences at just seven years old with her performance in *I Am Sam,* Dakota Fanning has continued to have a stellar career on the silver screen. She managed to carve out her place in Tinseltown despite her intense ethnic background (English, French, Irish, and German), proving you can do anything you set your mind to, no matter what bias you'll face on the basis of your ethnicity!

DIY: AGING!

How to Be More Gloria Steinem Than Gertrude Stein

It's a sad truth: women face constant scrutiny as they age, especially women in the media. We believe this is unfair to women and are determined to fight this injustice by celebrating women who age—gracefully!

Nobody is immune to aging,* but we tip our floppy summer hats to the strong women who have aged so beautifully (on the inside and out!) over the years. From Jane Fonda to Raquel Welch to feminist icon Gloria Steinem, we're constantly in awe of these brave women who have shown us that aging *isn't* a death sentence—it's something to be celebrated!

REALLY!

OUR PLEDGE

Keeping joy and beauty in your life is no easy task, and that's why 1 percent of the proceeds from every book we sell will go toward educating *all* women on how to age gracefully, because #Reductresscares about aging well.**

Of course, even us regular gals need to know how to prepare for our golden years, so let's take a look at what it really takes to exemplify the real, lasting beauty (on the inside and out!) that so uniquely showcases female strength—even if you're over forty.

Fact: Women who age gracefully are 40 percent less likely to fall into obscurity.

First, what does it mean to age gracefully? To answer this question, we looked into the very first Google search result for the answer. According to www.surgery.org, aging gracefully means "to do whatever is necessary to stride into your older years with confidence."

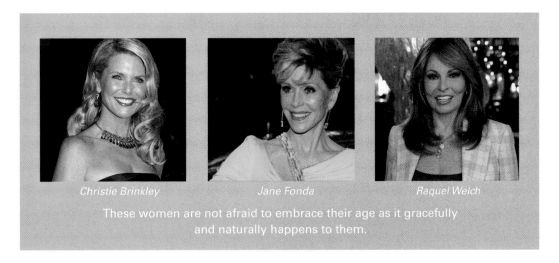

Christie Brinkley   Jane Fonda   Raquel Welch

These women are not afraid to embrace their age as it gracefully and naturally happens to them.

---

* Unless you are a man and happen to be a silver fox; in which case, e-mail us! SeekingSilverFoxes@gmail.com. Thanks!

** Proceeds will go toward asking gracefully aging women, "How do you do it?"

HOW TO AGE LIKE A FRENCH WOMAN— WITH SCARVES!

Have you ever seen an old French woman without a scarf? No. Aging French women know that the easiest, most effortless way to hide sagging neck skin is to throw on a scarf. French women are masters of disguise. They have to be to keep their husbands from flaunting their young mistresses too freely. So as those lines set in, throw on a scarf! *Très chic!*

Hey, we *love* striding with confidence, so sign us up for whatever is necessary! Overall, it looks like the main things are staying thin, having gorgeous eyes, still wearing makeup, and occasionally stepping out in a bikini to *let bitches know*. Tight!

In addition to looking and feeling confident, aging confidently also happens to be one of the signature goals of feminism. Why wouldn't you, as a woman who loves her body and her self, make your inevitable decline as graceful as possible?

Fact: Young people are three times more likely to care about those who have aged gracefully and effortlessly.

Aging gracefully should look effortless, and sometimes that can take a lot of work. As long as you're the gracefully aging type, these things should come naturally to you. Your daily yoga practice, lots of laughter, and green juice or a spell from the Old Country should keep you looking *and* feeling young for years to come. That way, the members of the local Girl Scout troop will fight each other to listen to your stories! You're the queen of the nursing home!

How to Age Gracefully

Although it's hard to know *exactly* how some women have maintained their good looks over the years,[*] these women give us faith that we too can be beautiful, inspiring, and a reminder

---

[*] It can't be *all because of the juice,* but then again, maybe it is??

to other older women that they should have tried harder. We consulted several more Google search results to find out exactly what these extraordinary women did to cultivate an ageless beauty, and here's what we found.

Have a positive attitude!

If you have already consulted a board-certified surgeon, one other way to age gracefully is to have a positive attitude! Women with sunny dispositions age more gracefully, because they don't waste all that negative energy *blaming* people or the media for their own failure to age correctly. Aging beauties like Suzanne Somers swear by the effects of a positive attitude, which keeps them smiling—on the inside *and* out. You wouldn't have to blame yourself in the first place if you just had a *positive attitude.* Try it on; you might like it! This does not involve surgery.

Enjoy a glass of wine!

Some of the oldest women alive today credit their longevity to a glass of red wine every day. What a fantastic way to enter decline! Just make sure you only have one glass, though! Two or more glasses will probably kill you. You may be graceful, but you are still old!

OUR AGE-DEFYING GREEN JUICE RECIPE

We've talked to some of the oldest and hottest celebs in Hollywood and found *the* recipe for a killer green juice guaranteed to keep you aging gracefully like a wise old skinny oak tree:

1 stalk celery
3 large kale leaves, washed
1 teaspoon lemon juice,
    freshly squeezed
The blood of an infant
3 wisps virgin's hair
    (blond preferred, obvs)
1 tablespoon spirulina
Dash of positive energy
Good vibes, to taste
Plastic surgery (optional)

WILL *YOU* AGE GRACEFULLY?

Not everyone is equipped to age gracefully, so here are a few key questions to ask yourself now in case you can save yourself some time and just give up now.

Did your mother age gracefully?

Just like the genetic indicators of how you're going to die, your mother is the best indicator of how gracefully you're going to age. Is your mother a Jane Fonda type or more of a Marlon Brando? If the latter, we're sorry, girl! You can't choose your mom, but you *can* blame her for all your problems in life.

Are you committed to a lifetime of healthy living?

If you're not committed to a full, long life of living well, eating well, and the occasional cosmetic procedure, then you're not ready to age gracefully. Are you up for being a bold, bad, beautiful older woman?!

Do you have a positive attitude?

Like we said, having a positive attitude is undoubtedly the most important factor in your likelihood to age gracefully. People with a positive attitude have fewer wrinkles, more friends, more money, and more sex appeal than their unhappier counterparts. So you have a positive outlook on life, right? Don't lie! You're only cheating yourself.

If you answered no to any of these questions, effortless graceful aging just might not be in the cards for you.

Eat spaghetti!

Beautiful former actress Sophia Loren swears by eating a full plate of spaghetti every day to keep herself looking—and feeling—hot as shit. Literally nothing but a plate of pasta and a great attitude has kept her looking like a spritely young woman well into old age. Finally we are already doing something right without even trying. We love you, Sophia!

If all else fails, BAG! (Be a Grandma!)

If aging gracefully just isn't a priority for you, you should try being more positive! And if you can't manage that, you can always go full-grandma. Instead of disappearing into obscurity, going full-BAG will allow people to take you more seriously when you're old. Everybody loves grandmas! As a grandma, you can make the most of your twilight years by inspiring young women with meandering advice and quirky sayings. If you're famous, you can even play some of your greatest acting roles as a wise old sage imparting advice to a younger, more fertile woman.

You can do this because grandmas *can say whatever the fuck they want.* Fostering a deep sense of poetic wisdom or just saying whatever the fuck you want will help keep you relevant in conversations with your granddaughters or the media. You can speak entirely in riddles, and people will still take care of you! Look at Judi Dench in her last five films—we can't understand a word she's saying, but she looks amazing while she's doing it! What a BAG!

HOW TO TAKE UP MORE SPACE, BUT NOT *TOO* MUCH SPACE

Men love tiny girls. But guess what, men. Most real women have curves, *and* fill seats, *and* use the armrest (or at least half of it, if that's okay). We want to say to men, "We're here in the room. You can literally see us," without being too annoying. Here's how to assert yourself by taking up more space in the room without being a total man about it.

Wear a wide-brimmed hat!

Wearing a wide-brimmed hat says, "Step aside, patriarchy—I'm all *over* the place!" Making feminist statements with tasteful hats is a nice way to be assertive in public places, but in a soft, feminine way. Show the world that you don't take no for an answer, especially when it comes to asking if the store has a bigger hat.

Womanspread (but not too much).

Men are always manspreading their legs all over the place—in the subway, on a plane, in our beds. So it's time for us to do the same! Just don't let your womanly guilt and overachieving nature get the best of you. You don't need to womanspread everywhere all the time, and there's no "right" way to do it. You know what? This is already getting a little exhausting. An easier solution might be to just cross your legs. Crossed legs say, "I'm a strong, confident, sexy woman with a vagina-hole. Please don't touch my vagina-hole. I'm sorry I'm here." Nailed it!

Lean in, but with a little bit of tasteful cleave.

There's nothing the world* loves more than an eager, fresh-chested woman who's heading toward horizontal. Give yourself and other women a leg up by asserting yourself physically

---

* I.e., men.

into workplace conversations while smiling and being delicious to look at. Female colleagues will thank you for giving them the courage to also speak cheerfully while wearing figure-flattering outfits. Just don't overstep your bounds by being negative or whiny, like pointing out a massive accounting error you discovered.

Do pelvic thrusts, but in reverse.

A secret assertion tool of successful businessmen is to take a broad stance with legs apart, hands on hips, and dicks thrust as far forward as possible, ideally into a seated colleague's face. So stand like a man! Just make this move slightly more palatable and feminine by thrusting your butt out instead of your vagina. By backing it up into the meeting, you're still leaning into the conversation with your pelvis, while showing off some more feminine assets. Trust us, your male colleagues will love how empowered you are!

Sit up straight, with your head cocked to the side!

We know it sounds crazy, but you don't always have to lay limp and sunken down in your chair during meetings so as not to block people's view. You can sit up, tall and strong—you deserve to be here too! You just don't want to come across as "aggressive," "abrasive," or "fully awake," so it's good to cock your head to the side with a look of quiet inquisitiveness. This stance shows men you're really getting involved in the discussion by paying attention to what they're saying, while still looking cute, like a puppy hearing an unfamiliar sound. Aww! Go you!

Build muscle (mentally).

Women should be allowed to be physically strong and have the physical mass that men do. Unfortunately, you probably don't want to go up a dress size and change your whole wardrobe. Not to mention, nobody likes a girl who's too "built." Who are you, an MMA fighter? Pack on some mental muscle by doing word games or Sudoku! Fierce! Your brain waves will be all up in this piece!

Noisespread (quietly).

Ever heard a man talk on the phone? Of course you have. You can probably hear one now! They shout into those things like they're commanding the D-Day invasion, even if the convo is just about what they did that weekend. You too deserve to take over the room with a private conversation no one else is interested in. Just know that your high-pitched female tone can be really grating, so you might want to bring it down to a five. Plus, you don't want the person on the other end of the phone to think you're mad, even if he *did* just break off your engagement. No one likes a yelly girl!

It can be hard for women to get used to taking up space, both physically and in conversation. That's why it's important to really get out there and announce your presence without apology, but also in an attractive way that men can get behind. If you find that men are put off by you no matter how much space you take up, you can always leave society and become a shut-in. It's just not worth setting women back by being obnoxious!

Plinky Checks In

Well, well, look here, I know that smug look!
"I've read up through part 2 of this book!
That means I'm a fem'nist, one hundred percent!"
You silly bill-billy, that's only a dent!

Ho ho, hee hee,
Keep going, my pretty!
I killed a man in 1973,
And they can't prove it was me—
    I'm imaginary!

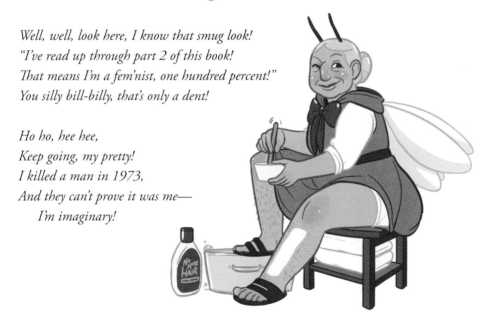

 DISCLAIMER

Disclaimer: Again, the murder thing is almost certainly a lie. She's super inspiring apart from the crime lies! Promise!!

WOMEN AT WORK!

Leaning In

I don't just work it.
I flip it, lean in, and reverse it.

I lead your ass,
This spin class,
Ride first class,
Sandberg/Kardash.

You Keeping Up with us?
You can eat our dust.

Laid the agenda,
'n' crudité platter,
My lady pockets
Getting fatter.

Working lunch, working dinner,
Working drinks, got two sitters.

Sittin' at that table
Got more pressure than you,
More papers than you,
Fax, fax like you don't care (I know you care).

My personal brand is money, honey.
Your glass ceiling is my cash feeling.

Have it all. Skirt size small. Conference call in my cubical.

SAINT HAVE-IT-ALL

PATRON SAINT OF LEANING IN

WORK IT!

#yesallwomencanworkit

Thanks to Rosie the Riveter and her retro-chic girl gang, you now have the right to have a job. A *real* one! Like, for a paycheck and everything! These days, women can achieve whatever they set their minds to. But just because you're *working* doesn't mean you're *working it*. Look in the reflective surface of your marble desk and ask yourself, "Are you working it?"

For the uninitiated, *working it* is the technical business term for being a hot, well-dressed businesswoman who knows how to flaunt her assets *and* close deals. It means wearing the *shit* out of a power dress while accomplishing every single one of your career and personal goals. It means looking good on paper, and even better when you bend over to pick up a stack of paper. And you better *believe* it involves a hefty dose of sass!

Does all of this sound unfeminist to you? Don't worry. As feminists, we're reclaiming the right to look good in the office. Our mothers only dressed to satisfy their male bosses, but today we *are* the bosses. The men we dress to satisfy work for *us*! And while working it does require a lot more from us as women, in the streets *and* folding sheets, *real* feminists are loving every minute of it. After all, we aren't wearing girdles and cleaning the house anymore. We're wearing Spanx and hiring a cleaning lady. That's feminism!

Make no mistake, the patriarchy still has a stranglehold on the workplace. Women only hold 14 percent of all the executive positions in America, and that is *not* okay. The good news is that women are making giant power lunges* forward every day. It's finally cool for women to love to work, and to make money, and to spend that money on sick outfits for work. We're leaning in all the way to the bank. And then straight to Ann Taylor. Sales don't last forever!

So we all know that women can have just as much impact in the workplace as

> ## WOMEN WHO HAVE IT ALL
>
> We understand it can be daunting to start your journey toward having it all, but rest assured, there are women out there who are making working it work for them. If you don't have a model for having it all in your own life, here's a list of absolutely perfect feminist examples of women who have it all:
>
> Kelly Ripa
> Clair Huxtable
> Maria from *Sesame Street*
> Charlotte Pickles
> The Nanny (just not all at once)
> Carol Brady (minus the job)
> Lorelai Gilmore (almost!)

---

*Don't our butt muscles look good?

men can and that it's just as important to look powerful as it is to feel powerful. But why? Let's face it: women have to look good in order to get ahead, and though it isn't fair, it's literally the only way to get more women to the top of the corporate ladder. Sure, you could march into work wearing a sweat suit and do things the hard way. Have fun slamming into the glass ceiling! If you want people to respect you and listen to your ideas, you have to walk the corporate walk—backward, and in heels!

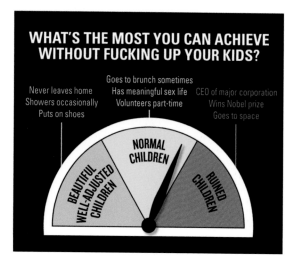

In other words, now it's what's on the outside that counts. That's why we support women in STEM heels, which look great paired with a sleek pencil skirt and loose blouse, behind a desk or in a boardroom! With a strong feminist look as detailed in the previous section, you cannot be ignored. But now that you're in the workplace, there are a host of other challenges to contend with.

You must have it all.

Why does it matter how you #workit in the workplace? Because looking impossibly good and working impossibly hard are the first steps to *having it all.* There are a lot of ways to have it all, but if you're reading this, it's safe to say you're not doing any of them.*

First, being a feminist in the working world means it's your responsibility to dispel stereotypes about women. If you are simply a mother, you make women look bad by implying that that is all we can aspire to be and that the whole women's movement was a waste of baby-making time. If you pursue your career without having children, you make feminists look like cold-hearted, cold-wombed Disney villains who could never appreciate the love of a child.

Are you moving up the ladder at a fast-growing company? That's fine, but someone else is doing all that while raising two beautiful kids both named Hunter. *That* woman is the face of feminism.

"But wait," you ask. "What if I don't want to be a mother, or what if I am a mom and hate leaving my kids at day care? What if I tried to achieve a perfect balance, and it didn't work?"

---

* Women who have it all don't have time to read; they're too busy having it all!

That's totally fine! You're allowed to do that. Just hop in your time machine that goes back to the Stone Age or fast-forward to a future where we're all robots. Go on, get out of here!*

Create your own personal brand!

Ready to have it all? Great! But before you pitch yourself to the shark tank of corporate America, you have to develop your *personal brand*. Your personal brand is like a pared-down cartoon version of yourself who wears the same outfit and the same three accessories and always says the same catchphrase. Think of the shinier parts of yourself.** Do you like to occasionally wear heels in bright, playful colors? Make that your thing, *every* day! Do you like to wear fun seasonal and topical*** nail art? Keep it up, *always*! Can you tolerate a lot of liquor? Continue!

Trust us, your superiors will definitely start to take notice. Kim Kardashian is a great example of a woman who found her brand and ran with it. She took her love for taking selfies, committed to it mercilessly, and has now become the human epitome of the selfie. You too can take a quirky e-mail signature or a clever mug and turn it into a distinctive trademark that will ensure you never get mistaken for Ruby, the former intern who overwatered the plants that one time.

It's important that your personal brand be multifaceted. Find your personal brand by selecting one word from each of the three columns below and combining them. Remember: you want to make sure your brand is edgy and unique, yet safe enough for everyone to like it, especially your boss.

Glitzy	Implants	Goddess
Hot	Pies	Mom
Fierce	Cupcakes	Lady
Skinny	Girl	Cocktails
Fastest	Service	Streaming
Slutty	Bathroom-Crying	Lisa
Stunning	CrossFit	Patriot
Plus-Size	Princess	Warrior

---

* If you don't have access to a time machine, you're gonna have to choose to have it all, which you don't really have a choice about if you want to win this thing.

** No, we're not talking about your oily forehead.

*** Try spelling E-L-E-C-T-I-O-N-!-! out on your nails!

Pull yourself up by your boobstraps.

When it comes to your job, are you really getting it done? Not just some of it, but, like, *all* of it? Like even stuff that's other people's jobs? The modern-day feminist is the Olivia Pope of the workplace. She's an expert multitasker, knower of all office secrets, conveyer of urgency, haver of an affair with a very powerful man, and general fixer of everyone else's messes. She may have started from the bottom, but now she's waaaay up here. So if there's a deadline tomorrow and your coworkers don't seem to be really *feeling* the pressure, you should be the one to go around to every desk and remind them of the project's importance, while also reminding them of the importance of "loyalty." Just because you're not the boss doesn't mean you can't be a bo$$ bitch!

Climb.

Now that you've shown your leadership skills, it's only fair that you should start climbing that ladder, leaning in (and up), and chainsawing through that glass ceiling like the female antagonist in a horror movie. Every feminist should set her sights on a top-dog role in

BAN "BASIC"!

Who decided to label inoffensive crowd pleasers with the horrible term "basic"? This hurtful term has gotten in the way of female fashion advancement, making sensible staples into something to be ashamed of. This is especially harmful when you realize the power in certain "basic" looks that we love! Sure, a lot of us may be rocking a few simple pieces, but perhaps that's because they're *classic,* not basic. After all, who doesn't look good in an all-greige outfit at the office? Seriously, it took us a lot of time to find a pencil skirt, flats, chiffon top, and statement necklace, all in the *exact* same shade of greige. So don't you dare try to take this away from us! We look good. And what may appear "simple" is actually really difficult to accomplish, FYI.

FOR REALS

OUR PLEDGE

One percent of the proceeds of this book will go toward banning "basic."

whatever company she's working for, even if it's as the curator of her own Etsy store. Also, just 'cause you're climbing doesn't mean you should look like a backpacker. No flats!*

It's a shark-eat-shark** world out there for women in the workplace. So make sure you bring your feminist tool kit and sewing kit*** along, and get it, girl! Men may be born naturally empowered, but as women we have to empower *ourselves*. So what's it gonna be? Are you gonna let a few stress donuts and a pair of comfortable shoes get in the way of *women's advancement*?

PROTECTING YOUR BODY OF WORK

Thanks to careful styling and hard work, but mostly styling, today's women are a force to be reckoned with professionally. But despite all of our progress, women still have hazards to overcome in the workplace, especially in offices that use fluorescent lighting.**** Men have to worry about progressing too quickly, but it should come as no surprise that women's greatest professional concern is how they look. Did you know that women who are overweight are 107 times as likely to be passed over for a promotion? Don't let that be you!*****

Unfortunately, the modern workplace is filled with hazards that can trap unsuspecting women in *dangerous* situations, like free pizza or gift cards to the Cheesecake Factory in lieu of a bonus. Here's a list of some common caloric traps set for women in the workplace.

Coworker-Provided Snacks

Sure, it seems fun when Doreen brings in donuts for National Donut Day or gets a birthday cake for Marie, but today's treat could be tomorrow's lost opportunity. How are you going to lift up other women if you're still a marketing assistant in five years? Do a smoothie demo in the office kitchen with fun little sample servings for all, and let Doreen know that she will not bring you down, not today.

Office Vending Machines

We pray you don't have one of these in your workplace for the same reasons listed above. Vending machines were created by men to keep you from walking outside or opting for a

---

* Heels look even better in rough terrain. See Bryce Dallas Howard in *Jurassic World*.
** We are OBSESSED with *Shark Tank*!
*** Seriously, this is so helpful if you lose a button on that blouse.
**** Like the overuse of air conditioning, this is yet another plot against women in the workplace.
*****You can't get to the top without playing by the rules! Unless you're a man. See also: Hillary Clinton.

handful of almonds. Everything in there will bloat you up or drag you down. No good for someone who's on a deadline and in a pencil skirt! If you give in to the vending machine, you can kiss your career good-bye. Instead, bring in preportioned carrots and celery in plastic bags, every day. This is a healthy choice that will garner respect and will strike fear in the hearts of everyone around you.

Lunch

When all the boys at the office are hitting the steakhouse for a power lunch, run the other way! Even if you go for the wedge salad, its bleu cheese and crumbled bacon could send you back to the mailroom. We can't afford to have one less woman in middle management! Instead, eat a meal replacement bar while walking, like a normal woman!

Happy Hour

By far the most tempting and the easiest to fall victim to at the end of a long day, the office happy hour is just as much a caloric landmine as all the foods listed above. If you simply *must* have your drink and blow off steam with the gang, opt for a vodka and seltzer and then run five miles the next morning before work.

Black Coffee with a Packet of Artificial Sweetener

A zero-calorie pick-me-up seems like the perfect beverage for a woman looking to get ahead. *But buyer beware!* Both caffeine and sweeteners may actually boost your appetite, leading to overeating and probably cancer. If you value your job, reach for a glass of room-temp lemon water in the morning instead of your usual cup of joe. Your pension will thank you!

SUPPORTING OTHER WORKING WOMEN

While you're overcoming the odds by watching your waistline, don't forget your solemn responsibility to look out for other women. As a successful woman on the way to having it all, it's your responsibility to be a mentor to other working women. Remember, all successful women got their start when they were mentioned by Oprah on an episode of her show. You can be someone else's Oprah by supporting them with these helpful behaviors.

Support other female-driven businesses.

Helping other women actually helps you. For example, things didn't really gel creatively at our office until we hired a full-time hair braider. Now Morwenna's able to get paid for her intricate braids, and we're able to get more work done, because our hair is pulled beautifully back from our faces. Not to mention it's easier to collaborate when everyone looks cute!

Buy a crate of coconut water.

It's nature's purest kind of water! Your male coworkers probably won't touch it for fear of catching estrogen, while you and your female coworkers will be up to your eyeballs in life-changing electrolytes. Also, sipping a box of coconut water is a great way to establish dominance over other women you're supporting.

Make a custom office playlist.

Got all hands on deck for a big presentation? Nothing gets everyone psyched for a collaborative project like a sick beat. Encourage other women in your workplace to put their best foot forward by throwing together an empowering playlist full of Rihanna, Aretha, and Alicia Keys.[*]

Make up fun nicknames for the group of women in the office.

The guys have their boys' club, so you women need to stick together and show them how much fun you're having. Call them your "girlies" or "the Wednesday salad gang" or your "business babes." When you have each other's backs in a fun, catchy way, the men in the office will start to take all of you more seriously.[**]

Sneak out early for mani-pedis.

Nothing combats the workplace patriarchy like verbally bashing it. Have a gab sesh over mani-pedis, so that the younger women in your office know that you *really* feel what they're

---

[*] Bonus: this playlist will not work on heterosexual men.
[**] Even Sara, who put regular dish soap in the office dishwasher.

going through. You've been there with Todd's gropey massages, and expensing these manis to his corporate account is the *best* revenge!*

Let other women know when they're working it.

Is another woman really killing it this week with her houndstooth skirt and Burberry handbag? Tell her! If we don't let other women know when they're excelling in the workplace, they may never know whether they're really doing a good job.**

Do not sleep with Brian.

Also—and we know this one's so, so, so hard—but do your best to never kiss or sex or wink at Brian. He's already hooked up with, like, three other girls in the office, and if you're going to band together you *cannot* let Brian come between you. If you already hooked up with Brian, like, literally last night, try your best to prevent any of the other women from doing so by explaining how weird he was after and that the sex wasn't even that good, really. Now, get out there and support your fellow ladies!

THE CONSEQUENCES OF NOT HAVING IT ALL

Every woman should strive toward having it all. Why settle for anything less? The dream is readily available for women with courage, persistence, and half an ounce of self-respect. Not having it all is not only a threat to feminism at large; it also has dangerous repercussions for your personal life as well. Studies have shown that not having it all can lead people to worry about what they're doing with their life. You don't want to make people worried, do you?***

In this golden age of feminism, some women still fall into the easy trap of having just *some* of it. But women have been given special lady gifts that men do not have, and therefore it is our duty to use them, all of them, at the same time. Take caution and heed the poor examples of the following women who had a little, but just didn't make it work enough to have it all. They may profess to be happy, but are they really?

---

* That won't get you flagged as "difficult."

** It's especially important to give impressionable young women and interns the validation and support they need in the workplace.

*** Too late.

The Shackled Soccer Mom

> "Spending forty hours a week in an office just never agreed with me. Now that my husband makes more than enough money to support our family, I'm happy to stay home. I love being a mom."
>
> — LUCY GOLD, *stay-at-home mom*

Yikes, Lucy's life sounds like a Victorian tragedy! This could be you, toiling away at home without a single adult to converse with, if you don't find a way to juggle the work–life balance. And we can only imagine the unpolished outfits, lax hair,* and sad attempt at makeup you'll be sporting when you leave the house just to see other depressed moms like yourself. Remember, sadness is a choice.

The Lonely Office Spinster

> "My husband and I value our careers and enjoy frequent travel. Raising kids just never appealed to me. I'm happy to spend time with my nieces and nephews and then return to the freewheeling life I love."
>
> — JENNY CARLOTTA, *software implementation engineer, TechSystems Int'l, Inc.*

There's nothing that saddens us more than a woman who works all day and comes home to an empty home with no one to serve and take care of. Every strong working woman should have a daughter she can mold into someone even more successful than herself. Even if Jenny doesn't realize it now, she is destined for a dismal grandchildless future, with no one to rub those feet after decades of teaching seminars in heels.**

The Hollow Philanthropist

> "I don't have kids or a job in the traditional sense. My family is pretty wealthy, so I'm able to do charity work with underprivileged girls in third-world countries, helping them gain access to education. My life is so fulfilling, and I'm so happy."
>
> — TERESA LENZ *(nothing)*

Can a woman who doesn't work or birth even be considered a woman at all? Not a feminist woman, that's for sure. Poor Teresa. What a waste.

---

* Probably a ponytail, or worse—a clip.

** If you teach a seminar and want anyone to listen, it is imperative that you wear heels.

HELPING OTHER WOMEN HAVE IT ALL

If you see any of your friends or colleagues veering down the dark path toward not having it all, it's important to take on a mentorship role and help get them back on track. Every woman deserves to have it all, even if she went to a college you've never heard of.

Lead by example.

Keep a copy of *Lean In* on your desk, right next to a photo of your adorable family. At lunch, artfully reveal your corporate credit card, along with a photo of your son at his preschool graduation, tucked neatly into your Marc by Marc Jacobs wallet. Have an expensive titanium stroller shipped to your office and say to your secretary, "Kinda makes you want a baby, doesn't it?"

Play matchmaker.

Some women avoid having a family because they haven't met the right guy—someone who wants kids and would be a good provider. Just because Marcy says she "enjoys being single," doesn't mean you can't stage an accidental meeting with your handsome business-owner brother-in-law. She'll see!

Offer to help them with their résumé.

If your friend seems to insist on staying home with her kids, claiming she "doesn't miss working," just continually offer to help her work on her résumé. When she sees you typing up her professional accomplishments, she's sure to miss the thrill of the workplace. You can even send it out to a few places to get the ball rolling!

HOW TO APOLOGIZE FOR HAVING IT ALL

"Having it all" is an ideal we all strive toward, but few of us ever fully achieve, sort of like nirvana or a thigh gap. If you feel you have it all (or at least most of it), that's wonderful! Namaste, girlfriend! Now comes an important step in any female success: *playing it down*. Here's how to make sure the satisfactory work–life balance you've fought tooth and nail for doesn't make anyone resent you.

Say "Sorry" if someone walks in on you pumping breast milk at work.

Whether you're in your corner office or a designated lactation room, make sure to apologize to the young male intern who has never heard the sound of a breast pump before. As soon as he breezes in, say, "I'm sorry for making the best choice for me and my baby in a way that does not interfere with my work. I will switch to formula from now on." Toss the pump out the window in a show of good faith. Your intern will be speechless with gratitude!

Apologize to your baby for having a Ph.D.

Studies show that babies as young as two months old can tell when their mothers think they're better than everyone else. Even though she can't speak yet, it's good to start apologizing to your baby early, so that she can develop the apology part of her brain. As you rock her gently to sleep, whisper, "I'm sorry for being one of the leading chemical engineers in North America. That's super self-involved of me. I love you, baby." Then take your framed doctorate off the wall and replace it with any Anne Geddes photo where the babies look particularly sorry. You might have it all, but a judgy baby should not be one of them!

Pretend to miserably do paperwork during your daughter's recital.

You made sure to finish all your work early so you could be here, but don't let that balance show! You don't want the other dance moms to envy the look of total contentment in your eyes, so it's best to bury those eyes in a sheaf of paperwork. Shuffle a miserable amount of papers and scribble on them furiously, only glancing up at the show once or twice. It'd be nice to enjoy this special moment you worked so hard to be present for, but it would be even nicer to have your choices tacitly approved of by the near strangers in your midst. Get to work!!!

Weep over a picture of your children, even though they're in day care downstairs.

Let your coworkers see just how hard it is for you to be away from "your babies," who are currently being tended to in an excellent child-care facility on the fourth floor. Sure, you just spent a rainy three-day weekend indoors with the kids and are glad to be back around other adults, but that doesn't mean you can't use this opportunity to validate your childless colleagues' life choices. It's not like they have any idea your company provides a day care with a three-to-one child-to-caretaker ratio as part of its standard benefits package. If you want to show how sorry you are for having it all, let your salty tears fall on your kids' Little League photos as if they call the nanny "Mommy."

Whenever another PTA mom asks how old your kids are, stammer an incorrect answer.

Of *course* you know their ages—you're their mom! You even incorporated their birth dates into a meaningful geometric tattoo on your inner bicep. However, pretending to forget how old your kids are is a great way to confirm the suspicions of stay-at-home moms in your social group. When Leah's mom asks, "How old is your youngest?" manufacture a look of panic, tilt your head to the side, shift your weight to your other leg, shake your hair off your face, and mutter, "S-sevix. Six. Sevenish. Six or seven. Look, mind your business! I'm a working mom!! Oh God, I'm so sorry. So, so sorry." Not only will you succinctly apologize for maintaining your career while starting a family; you'll also assuage your own guilt at living a life otherwise free of guilt. Sevix it is!

Look like hell.

Wherever you are, it's important to look like garbage, even though you had no problem losing the baby weight and have a style that's neither matronly nor severe. Show your regret for making it work by turning your kemptness down a notch. Apply three honey-nut Cheerios onto your blazer before all presentations. Scream into a giant cell phone while picking your daughter up from school. Wet your blouse over both nipples as if to say, "My breasts yearn to nurse my ignored child," even if you *did* buy the pricier nipple shields. Being a physical wreck is the best way to say, "Sorry my life is baseline manageable."

Pretend to get super trashed off one beer with your friends.

So you and your partner's work schedules mesh perfectly, giving you both plenty of time to spend on your kids, careers, and social lives. Your friends, however, were kind of counting on your turning into an alien recluse once you gave birth. Surely you'd get lame on them! You'd smell like baby! You'd be all, like, grown-up and shit! If you're not a total buzzkill, their heads will spin—and not just because of the double IPAs!

Show them how *mommified* you are by getting "tanked" off one beer after your next kickball game. They'll have a great time carrying you to the bathroom, loading you into a taxi, and saying, "All it took was nine months off booze and she's a lightweight again!" You'll know the act was convincing if they completely forget you adopted.

Say "I'm sorry" every hour, on the hour.

Just in case your happy life has made anyone else feel bad in the past few minutes, say, "I'm sorry" out loud every hour. To be on the safe side, set an alarm on your phone so you don't forget. Having it all is nice and all, but that doesn't give you license to throw it in everyone's faces! Be considerate of other people's bitterness and apologize on a regular basis. But also make sure to occasionally miss a scheduled blanket apology; you don't want people knowing how in control you are of your busy schedule!

Remember, being an active participant in your children's lives while maintaining your identity as an adult and establishing your professional legacy is no excuse to enjoy yourself! Apologize regularly for having it all, and who knows? Maybe you'll get through life without being such a showoff!

Mamala Breast Pumps Let You Have It All!
(IN THE BACK ROOM)

You're a working woman, and thanks to modern technology you can spring back into the office after that ten-day maternity leave while still nourishing your baby! Being a team player shouldn't cost you the ability to produce that invaluable, precious, never-a-drop-to-be-lost liquid gold oozing from your boobs. Just grab one of these Mamala pumps during every break you're contractually allowed, find a dark, dark corner, and pump away, Mama! Remember, you cannot have it all without a breast pump!

Mamala Breast Beat with Signature Suck ($998)

Pump your boobs to completion with the Breast Beat's patented Colostrum-flo technology. Mamala's highest-end pump, the Breast Beat is used by female CEOs the world over. This heavy-duty model weighs in at 44 pounds, enough to show the boys in the boardroom who's really boss! Just don't let the higher-ups see it, or they might wonder if you're "still pulling your weight." And rest assured, it's loud enough for everyone to wonder what the hell's going on in there!

Mamala Business Tripper Light ($879)

At just 20 pounds, the Business Tripper fits easily into any first-class luggage bin. So you can take your business to Tokyo while that C-section's still healing and bring back the best souvenir of all—milk from your boobs—to the baby you've sort of bonded with. Its signature 30-decibel buzz will announce, "Something weird's going on in here, and you can't relate!"

Mamala Walk-and-Talk Boss Bitch ($699)

When you're crying due to exhaustion and rapid hormone fluctuations and changing out of another tear-and-breast-milk-soaked blouse, you'll be glad to have Mamala's lightest pump by your side. Weighing just 1 ounce, it squeezes milk slowly and steadily out of your breasts, throughout the day, into a colostomy-like bag that adheres to your leg. Easy. Its tinny vibrations will whisper, "Baby comes first, *but so does work!*"

With the right breast pump and the right hidden, closed-off, dark corner of the office, you'll be back to having it all in no time! And you thought being a working mom would be hard!

Feature: LINDA MARIE MAARTER, THE WOMAN WHO LITERALLY HAS IT ALL

Three months into her dream job as the Director of the Securities Commission of the National Security Agency for Women in Start-ups Helping the Homeless and Wildlife, Linda Maarter, mother of two, was facing the age-old question: Can women really have it all? Looking at the state of her life, we can only conclude that the answer is a resounding "Yes!" And if she can do it, anybody can! Here's her story.

After two well-timed births in between degrees, I found myself constantly torn between being a perfect mother, perfect employee, perfect friend, perfect wife, perfect yoga practitioner, and a *great* fuck. What a balancing act that was! But after my first meditation class ever, I realized the only challenge was *believing in myself*.

After all, I am just like you. I eat light, require only two hours of sleep a night, and can mysteriously siphon power from others to increase my own. When you're forced to draw on your own resources, you find that you can easily exceed all expectations. Who can't relate to that?

After celebrating my thirtieth birthday with the Obamas a few years ago, not even my dual M.B.A./Ph.D. could have prepared me for the feeling that struck: I missed my six-year-old son (who was home with a sitter). Even though I had recently edited a video of my favorite memories of his life and could watch it easily on my smartphone any time his darling face crossed my mind, a little pang of guilt pinged my woman-heart. Why couldn't I be spending time with him instead of dining with several heads of state, all while breast-feeding my youngest child underneath an effortlessly chic nursing cloak? These are the kinds of things that many working moms struggle with every day—and yet it's a problem that's so easily solvable!

Though I was having a marvelous time telling everyone about my hilarious first attempts to install green roofs in Caracas, I felt the siren call of my child. I did what any working mother would do—I left Barack, Michelle, and the cake they had designed in my image and Uber'd a helicopter home to pick up my son and fly back in time to beat Michelle in a lighthearted arm-wrestling match. Sure, it was unorthodox, but I'm sure we can all relate to the desire to put our kids first, even someone average and down-to-earth like Michelle. When we finally got home at 2 A.M., I put the kids to sleep and headed out for a quick 10K. A little exercise helps me relax before bed.

You see, I am living proof that women can have it all—if, by current medical standards, my current physical state is considered "alive." (My heart operates at a rate half that of the normal woman, which my physician speculates is to allow for extended hours of semi-wakefulness. I'm sure any woman could do this, with a little practice!)

The best thing to do is to focus on your strengths and avoid comparing yourself to others. Anyway, why is it that women waste so much of their precious time tearing down other women? Probably the long gestation period and preponderance of female hormones. Who am I to say—I'm not a doctor! I do have a doctorate (I got it while I was on maternity leave), but it's in dentistry, so it doesn't really count. I'm not one to exaggerate my accomplishments! Not like my husband, who goes around bragging about the time he saved Earth from that asteroid. Men, right?

But back to the matter at hand. What *is* having it all? It's about knowing when to take a break from a high-powered government position to go to the bathroom *and* call your ailing mother while sexting your husband, all at the same time. And also getting most of your energy from a lamp you invented that emits supercharged positive ions and mimics the sun's rays. I get so full if I'm not careful!

What *isn't* having it all? Having it all isn't about being a show-off or making other women feel like they aren't doing enough. It's about harnessing the magic that is available to all of us—a strong will, an ability to multitask, and a direct line of communication with at least eight heads of state. All you have to do is believe in yourself!

On that note, I want to emphasize that there is no way I could do what I do without my husband. He is my rock. But that doesn't make him any better at keeping the bathroom clean! The housekeeper I pay for does that, even though I also do that better than she does and sometimes fix her mistakes. She does not have it all, but she could if she just put her mind to it.

When I told my housekeeper that I was going to write this article, she said, "Did I clean the toilet to your liking?" She had not cleaned the toilet to my liking (but she was so close!). I am writing this as I rescrub the toilet while giving my husband the best blow job he's ever had and also doing our quarterly taxes.

So what does "having it all" *truly* mean? Perhaps we should focus less on the question and more on wherever you find joy, like, for example, this orgasm I'll be having for the next nine minutes, which I'm able to achieve through only one minute of digital stimulation.

WORK–LIFE BALANCE VS. LIFE–WORK BALANCE: WHICH IS RIGHT FOR YOU?

Every woman needs to find that proper mix of time spent at work and time spent at home. Whether you choose a work–life balance or a life–work balance is entirely up to you. Not sure which option sounds like the best fit? Here are a few real women who exemplify each femme balancing style. Read and see who you most relate to!

WORK–LIFE BALANCE
This is for career gals who also want to be moms.

TIME AT WORK 50% | TIME AT HOME 50%

"I stay home with Riley every Thursday, Saturday, and Sunday. That leaves me four days in the office. My mom watches the baby while I'm working, and my husband helps out too. It's not for everyone, but it works for our little family!"

—Keelin T., thirty-four, Bridgeport, Connecticut

Pros: Increased self-worth and a sense of purpose.

Cons: Increased stress, feelings of failure, and burnout.

Eighty-eight percent: The number of postlabor employees who feel they're disappointing both their children and their bosses.

LIFE–WORK BALANCE
This is for moms who also want to be career gals.

TIME AT HOME 50% | TIME AT WORK 50%

"I work Monday through Wednesday and Friday. That gives me three days at home with Connor. My mom babysits while I work, and my husband helps out too. It's not perfect, but it's close enough for us!"

—Yang I., forty-two, Washington, D.C.

Pros: Increased self-worth and a sense of purpose.

Cons: Increased stress, feelings of failure, and burnout.

Twelve percent: The number of working moms who feel they're able to satisfy both their children and their company.

It's important to choose the balance that's right for you. Don't make the mistake of attempting to juggle the wrong one!

REPRODUCING AT EXACTLY THE RIGHT TIME

As a strong woman it's up to you, and only you, to make sure no babies pop out of you at a bad time. You can't just expect men, the government, or your employer to help you with your decision, and why would you? Having a baby is your choice and your choice alone. It is also a choice that affects everyone around you and will continue to forever and ever, so don't be selfish about it, okay? It's totally your call, but your choice should also be to have kids at some point. The question is, when? Here are some situations in which you will know whether it is the right or wrong time for you to have a baby.

When you've just started a job: WRONG!

Are you gainfully employed in a new job you enjoy? This is the wrong time to have a baby. You risk prioritizing your child ahead of your career or vice versa, and every good feminist knows you have to *own* your feminism by achieving a heap of career successes before you can have a truly feminist child. Wait until you're just senior enough that coworkers will start to worry about your ability to reproduce, but not so senior that all your eggs have dried up.

Exception: You have frozen all your eggs and have a net worth of at least $5 million.

When you've just left a job: ALSO WRONG!

How do you expect to pay for a *baby* without insurance and maternity leave? What are you, some kind of monster?

Exception: You are married to a very successful Hollywood director who openly advocates for women's rights.

When you're happily married: RIGHT!

So you're finally married to the man of your dreams and everything is going great? The biggest mistake you could make at this point is to *not* have a baby. Happy couples who don't have babies risk sliding into a dark vice-filled abyss from which they can never return. Luckily, having a baby solves everything and keeps marriages on the straight and narrow, provided you have a man who wants you to have it and can financially and emotionally support your decision and that stubborn baby weight. It also helps if he's tall!

When you're single and don't run your own company: WRONG!

Do you think society is going to help you deal with the financial and emotional struggles of having a child? They're not. Unless you are the sole owner or CEO of your own corporation that you can model to conform to your needs as a mother, chances are you are *not* ready to have a baby.

When you're single and do run your own company: ALSO WRONG!

Seriously, who do you think you are?? Your tireless drive and corporate know-how will have completely eroded the layer of maternal fuzziness required for mommyhood. Babies like soft mommies with no backbone—you're too strong to have a baby! Meanwhile, employees will see the baby as a sign of your poor planning skills, and your authority will be undermined. Having a baby means you're weak! It's a lose-lose, and all you do is win. Nice try, Eve Jobs!

When you found a lightly used Bugaboo Chameleon 3 Classic Stroller on the sidewalk: RIGHT!

It's a sign from the universe! Find a baby and have it now!!

When you're just getting over a breakup: WRONG!

Do not make any rash decisions. Now is not the time for haircuts, relocations, or babies. Just put on your fave rom-com DVD and slow your shit down.*

When you're ready to date again: ALSO WRONG!

Are you starting to see the pattern here? You are frequently wrong.

When you have a beautifully styled nursery: RIGHT!

You're ready, girl. You're so ready.

---

* Womb Trigger Warning: Make sure your fave rom-com doesn't have any babies in it.

BABIES AT FORTY-THREE AND A HALF! THE NEW IDEAL

More and more women are finding that the best time to have a baby is at forty-three and a half years old. Your career is finally sufficiently underway, but you're not quite dead yet. Here are a few women who timed their babies perfectly:

"It wasn't until I was forty-three and a half that I had enough money to hire a full-time staff to raise and tutor my child. *That* was the right time for me."

—Paige, forty-three and a half, founder of Yogurt-Kook™ Frozen Yogurts

"I can't imagine having a kid before I was forty-three and a half. In my twenties I was so guy-obsessed. In my thirties I was only on the board of three companies. It wasn't until I hit forty-three and a half that I really started networking with people who had access to the right preschools."

—Janet, forty-three and a half, CEO of Yoglert™

"When you're young, you think you're invincible and that you'll be able to find a good doula and surrogate easily. Boy, was I wrong!"

—Dame Judi Dench, eighty, yogurt lover, shareholder in MeYogurt™

HER-SSENTIALS FOR A HOME OFFICE

Times have changed, and now a woman's place is barefoot in the *home office*! After decades of fighting to get out of the home and into the workplace, you've done right by your fore-mothers by bringing that journey back into the home. Talk about going full circle! Whether you're telecommuting to your cushy corporate job or simply selling your line of Bespoke Soaps,* working from home is the ultimate achievement for every cog in this capitalist

---

* B'soaps!

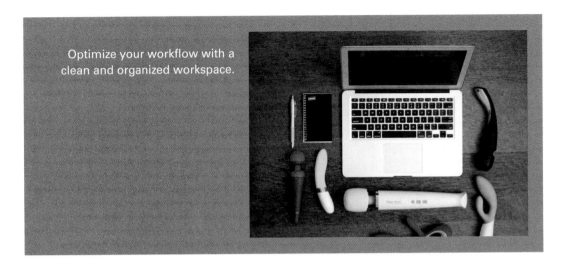

Optimize your workflow with a clean and organized workspace.

machine, and there's nothing more important than setting up your work space. It's not like you're going to be sitting around masturbating all day!

You won't, right? Promise? This won't be like last time, when all you did was masturbate a lot, right?

Great! Now that that's settled, here's everything you'll need to build the perfect feminist home office.

Spartan Pride Standing Desk

Working from home means you can finally be your best self! Start your massive life overhaul by picking up an obesity-busting, mind-focusing, life-fixing standing desk. This model from Spartan Pride allows you to raise your work space to your unique lady height, effectively disrupting your sedentary office hours and improving circulation in your lower body. Some people report noticeably increased blood flow to the pelvic area in as little as two weeks!

Guttfacher-Schlösser Massaging Office-Chair Cover

You need a massage! Standing for eight hours (not including masturbation breaks) has really taken a toll on your back, and this German luxury-electronics brand has just the product for you. Shiatsu rollers knead into three parts of your back, while heating pads vibrate at a speed of your choosing. Try to avoid the temptation to straddle your chair backward anytime you're feeling stressed. You're stressed now. But you're not doing *that* now.

Pond's Grove Water Dispenser

Okay, so you just rode your office chair for an hour. Big deal! You're adjusting to home-office life. Recreate old rituals and have your own water-cooler chat with your cat! He's your only coworker now, after all. You could even work naked; he wouldn't care! Just to prove a point to yourself, you're working naked all week! Make sure you stay hydrated during those long, audio-only Skype calls with this spring-water dispenser. Feel those bubbles release, sending powerful vibrations into your lower abdomen. Mmm. Wow. That's—strikingly nice . . . how does it know?

Hearasonic C-435 Wireless Headset

Okay, focus up. No more pleasuring yourself—got it? Back to business. When you made the leap to run a business out of your home, you pictured yourself wearing a nifty headset while pacing confidently across your carpet, sealing a deal with the greatest of ease, maybe even while sipping a mug of green tea. Sure, it'll mostly be used for Britney Spears lip sync routines, but that's beside the point! You deserve to feel sexy and feminine while handling several phone calls per week. Just make sure you hit the mute button if you use your massage chair during a conference call. You don't want everyone to think you spend all day masturbating, do you?

Buzzmatuzz Funny Bunny Vibrator

Okay, fine. Business is slow, and you deserve some self-love. You've earned that at least, if not any actual money. This is the vibrator made famous by *Sex and the City*, and it's no surprise: Carrie worked from home! The perfectly positioned rabbit ears will take care of the outer "customer interface," while the rotating pearls and vibrating shaft will "liaise with upper management." You can still bill a client for this! Just don't let this thing own you . . .

Office Parts Filing Cabinet

Back to work! You're the boss now, and being the boss means having the best possible secretary—yourself! This two-drawer model from Office Parts holds all your most important files, folders, and papers, even this old folder from college! Wow! Look at all these old papers and—huh, some photos fell out! Wow. Oh, *wow*. You sure were flexible back then!

Take a quick power lunch to reminisce about all the kinds of sex you were having back when you first got your business degree. It's important to connect with your roots!

A Laptop for Not-Porn

Okay, so maybe some breaks take longer than you think they will. Your desktop can't come with you to client meetings at coffee shops, so treat yourself to the portability of an ultrathin laptop. But before you take it out into the world, you should really test the machine's ability to connect to Wi-Fi by doing a quick Google search. How about something simple like, "John Cena butt movie scene slow motion" . . .

Kurashi Wizard Stick

God, that feels good.

Paper

Focus. The printer is *not* just for grinding against. You *cannot* keep sending fifty-page documents to print (just for the sake of absorbing those sweet, pulsating vibrations) unless there's paper in there. You're going to ruin your printer. Now come on, get a hold of yourself. No, not like that!!

Notebook

Listen to us, okay? This is your life. You choose how you spend it. Get your hands and electronics out of your crotch for one second and go buy a notebook. You can use it for keeping track of discussion items during a phone call, recording the progress of a specific project over time, journaling about how you feel working alone, journaling about your dreams, journaling about your fantasies, journaling about a young Dwayne "The Rock" Johnson bending you over a locker-room bench . . .

L'Petit Mimi Vibrator from Mais Oui

Yep, you're pretty much just masturbating now. Welcome home!

Feature: MEGYN KELLY: REPUBLICANS CAN RECLAIM FEMINISM TOO!

Don't let your politics get in the way of what you believe! Take it from Republican feminist Megyn Kelly, who shares her advice below.

It can be hard enough to be a Republican and a woman at the same time—try being a feminist too! Since women are statistically more likely to vote Democrat, it can be hard to find someone to go to brunch or the gym or to frext with if you believe in trickle-down economics or building a wall across the border with Mexico. But don't worry—now we have our own kind of feminism: *Republican feminism!*

Feminism used to be a big no-no for Republicans, but after enough time had passed, Republican women learned to appreciate the new freedoms they had, like wearing pants and not having to repent after sex. The day I arrived at FOX News, I scoffed at the smug white men in a way that was so familiar; almost *every* woman could get behind it. Finally, Republican women were slowly able to reclaim a piece of feminism on their own terms—*Republican* terms! Go get 'em, girls!

From Sarah Palin to Carly Fiorina, other strong women joined me in my quest, proving that women *really could* do things outside of the house, like enter the workplace, or have a career, or even shoot a moose if they wanted to. These women have shown that feminism is about standing on your own two feet—sometimes while pregnant and in heels—and not depending on the *government* to protect you. Thanks to these trailblazers, women have more choices than ever!

It can be hard for Republican women to negotiate their feminist beliefs with their political views, but that doesn't mean you can't have both! Remember, you can believe in yourself and your place in the world, but you don't have to vote for it. Here's how I combine my own special version of feminism with my core conservative beliefs.

(continued)

Take on feminist causes from thirty years ago.

Women fought long and hard for the right to vote and the right to work, so why stop there? 'Cause you're a Republican, that's why! Support art that shows the struggle for civil rights that we already won (like the novel *The Help,* or maybe the film *The Help*), so you can rest assured knowing that everything is okay now and if you had been alive back then you definitely would have supported the cause. Also, Jesus is a white man. Santa too.

Combat misogyny—as long as it isn't backed up by Christian beliefs.

If one of your colleagues uses a sexist term, call him out on it! But if he says he believes, as a Christian, that a woman's place is in the home, then just leave him alone. You can't mess with a person's belief system!

Donate to women's charities.

Whether it's a 5K run/walk to fight breast cancer or a bake sale to help poor teen girls buy sanitary pads, donating to women's charities can help you support women without bringing big government into their homes. Remember, women have to help themselves—and not by relying on wasteful public services.

If you work, make the workplace your cause.

Equal pay. Maternity leave. The sky is the limit, but you should aim a lot lower than that. The important thing is that you take a stand for *something,* even if it's something that literally nobody disagrees with. This is the best way to have integrity without having to work too hard for it.

If you're at home, be a mom-unteer!

One of the most important tenets of feminism is helping other women, so if you want to support women, just get out there and do it! Helping women directly, like driving them to hospital visits or making them food, is a great way to say "I helped women today" without having to add any laws or regulations that would make the government even bigger and more wasteful.

Sticking to the basics will keep you from the hard decisions that go against your values, and as long as you have money, you won't have to worry about any problems of your own (except for the meddling government!). In the end, remind yourself that we women are still a pretty niche demographic, and we can support each other without ruining the country like Obama did. Prove that you're not your *typical* Republican by joining the cause—like me, Megyn Kelly.

SUCCESSFUL BUSINESSWOMEN: OUR ROLE MODELS

It's not just men who are making it big in business anymore. The female business leaders below have proven that success is built on intelligence and hard work, no matter your gender. These inspiring titans of industry honed their personal brands and forged their own unique paths in the business landscape, defining new ways to achieve success as a woman. Here are their stories.

Kim Kardashian West: Seeker of Opportunities

Success story: "I started out doing a small indie film marketed toward a young male demographic, then expanded my efforts toward a female market."

Income streams: Ongoing television appearances, product endorsements, and fragrances.

Personal role model: "Andrew Carnegie. I try to channel his work ethic when taking selfies."

Plans for next quarter: A butt-portrait retrospective and a hands-free, bra-supported selfie stick.

Kris Jenner: Founder of an Empire

Success story: "I partnered with other brands to produce a series of commercial assets, each of which has performed remarkably."

Holdings: Kourtney, Kim, Khloé, Kendall, Kylie, and now Kanye.

Personal role model: "Steve Jobs. I admire his commitment to design and brand consistency, which is why all of my products start with a *K*."

Plans for next quarter: "I'm talking to surgical professionals about some personal image enhancements, and I'm in talks to acquire a former pro wrestler."

Khloé Kardashian: Brand Strategist

Success story: "I fell in love with the family business."

Personal role model: "Napoleon Hill. When they came to us with the nail-polish line idea, I just tried to believe I could achieve it."

Plans for next quarter: Marketing a guided drinking tour of the Hamptons led by a wax figure in her image.

Kendall and Kylie Jenner: Business Reinventors

Success story: "We were spending a lot of time in our sisters' closets and realized we wanted to be a part of that story."

Income streams: Social-media modeling, gifted automobiles.

Personal role model: "Jack Welch. The way he streamlined GE is the same attitude we have when getting dressed. Like, why wear so many layers?"

Plans for next quarter: A waist trainer for your lips.

As you can see, there is a wide range of she-moguls to look to for inspiration. Whatever your particular skills are, you can surely see yourself in one of these inspiring women in business. You *can* have what they have, with a clear vision, a conscientious attitude, and Photoshop!

Feature: JANET HUGHES, THE WOMAN WHO DOESN'T ASPIRE SO THAT OTHERS CAN!

Self-appointed assistant office manager Janet Hughes has an inspiring story of not aspiring her way to the middle. Here's her story of overcoming the odds and finding her place in life (somewhere near the bottom), so she could help other women rise to the top.

I'm a team player, and I know that sometimes you have to take one for the team. While everyone is out on the playing field of their careers, I'm the one on the sidelines with orange slices and Capri Sun, ready to shout out support whenever possible. That's why I choose to take a different role at the private equity firm where I was hired right out of business school—assistant office manager. After years of being taught how to play with the big dogs, I finally had a role where I could support other women without getting in their way.

Now, you might be wondering why I declined a coveted position at a great company right after finishing my M.B.A. at Wharton, and here's why. For years, women were told to "lean in" and "sit at the table." But imagine if everybody sat at a table and leaned in at the same time. We'd all be bumping elbows and talking over each other, because nobody would know who is supposed to just smile and nod and make sure everyone who wanted a drink had one. That's not my idea of a nice table!

That's why, rather than voice my ideas about targeted media strategy, I focus on sweeping crumbs off the table and keeping the water jug filled during meetings. The benefits of these simple support moves are plain to see. Ever since I made those my responsibilities, my superior, Lindsay, has gotten three promotions. Now there is a new "senior" office manager above me, Shannon. She's great! Very young, but has lots of great ideas about seasonal decorating. We make a great team, so long as she's the captain.

You see, there's only so much room in the working world for women, and I don't want to take one slot from someone who really deserves it, even if I am fluent in four languages.

I had a lot of aspirations growing up—lawyer, doctor, human-rights activist—and though I'm certified to do all of these things, it never felt comfortable to me. Eventually, I realized that this ol' girl was never really meant to take the spotlight, or even the chorus, or any part in the play whatsoever. There has to be somebody there to clean up the stage afterward.

I've actually found that aspiring less has been sort of freeing. I have more time to clean up after my kids, cook for my husband, and exercise. But not too much exercise, because that front-row spot at SoulCycle belongs to Sherry. Go, Sherry!

Some have suggested that I should go into nonprofit work to use my talents to help other people, but I feel like that would really just make it all about "me," you know? Like, "Oh, look at Janet, trying to show off at how good she is at saving the lives of millions of children." Let someone else take the credit for good works for once! Plus, I'm way over-qualified. There's probably someone out there who is a much better fit for that kind of fun.

Anyway, if you're a working woman ready to embark upon a professional career path, I support you! I will do whatever it takes to get you where you want to go, but I refuse to take any credit for helping you. Trust me; I don't deserve it!

FOOT STOMPS AND OTHER PERCUSSIVE METHODS THAT LET 'EM KNOW WHO'S BOSS

It can be hard for women to make an impression in the workplace. We need to stand taller, work harder, and be better than our male colleagues in order to get ahead. But there's also another trick for getting their respect and attention. Making noise! We're not talking about your usual vocal fry and disruptive laughter—the methods below tap into a more primitive form of posturing: violent percussion. So slam some stuff and be the dominating force your company desires. You'll own the room and look like a boss!

Foot Stomp

When someone labels one of your ideas "bad," stomp right out of the room. Office stomping is yet another area where a sturdy set of heels can really make a difference. Your coworkers won't be able to ignore your strong and purposeful presence, and your name is sure to come up in the next discussion about who to consider for promotion.

Dropping a Stack of Papers on a Desk

Are you miffed about not receiving credit for all the work you're getting done? When you deliver that stack of proofread invoices to another employee's desk, make sure to hold it high above the desk and then let it drop down with a heavy thud. They'll be sure to thank you *now*.

Door Slam

If you've encountered a particularly egregious injustice in the workplace, such as not receiving an invite to a particularly important meeting due to your "disorderly conduct," "uncivil manners," and "inexplicable stomping," it's time to pull out the big guns and draw from the tools you utilized as a put-upon teenager. Enter the room mid-discussion, say, "Oh, I guess I'm not supposed to be here," and then leave with a forceful slam of the door. The team will see that you're not afraid to make waves in *this* office.

Chewing Gum Loudly

Chewing gum with your mouth open while other people are speaking to you is a great way to let them know that they're not the boss of you and you're not threatened by them at all. Don't let them think it was an accident. You're doing this on *purpose*. Now *you* have all the status, and they look childish.

Pencil Drums

Some people think that only boys can have fun. Show them that you, a woman, also have a sense of humor by making your desk your own personal drum kit and banging away like an animal in between phone calls. Your carefree vibe tells people you're doing well at your job. Noise registered equals status asserted.

Don't be shy if you come up with your own percussive techniques. Just ask yourself, "Would a man do this?" Yes. A man would do *anything* to get ahead, and so should you.

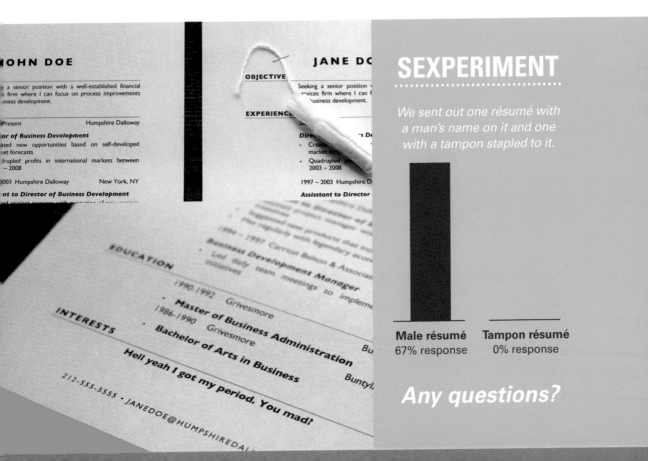

SEXPERIMENT

We sent out one résumé with a man's name on it and one with a tampon stapled to it.

Male résumé
67% response

Tampon résumé
0% response

Any questions?

Peep Pantiliners

Women are #unstoppable.
Your bladder-control problems #arent.

Women are strong. Women are tough.
Women are beautiful.

At Peep, we know that women have the power to do amazing things, even if they just peed a little.

Peep Pantiliners are committed to celebrating women who are powerful.

Don't let anybody tell you that you can't do something just because you're a woman. You have the power to overcome your obstacles, with a pantiliner that saves you from that little bit of pee that just dribbled out during a particularly devastating sneeze.

Pantiliners aren't just for incontinent old people anymore.

When we asked a group of girls aged twelve to sixteen how they felt about themselves, they said they felt terrible. That's why Peep is devoted to boosting the confidence of girls like these, especially when they have a period accident. Their growing bodies are leaking terrible, unspeakable things through their vaginas without any warning. No matter what's seeping out down there, we are committed to teaching girls how to have confidence and *love themselves just the way they are.*

It's proven that girls with self-confidence and reliable panty protection do better in school, are more likely to play sports, and are more likely to walk away from an abusive relationship, no matter how much pee came out.

You have the power to shape the future, even in cases where your period goes away and then kind of comes back without any warning.

It's your right to have a weird discharge that you think might be an STD but is probably normal.

Women deserve to laugh more, even if it makes them pee more. That's why we make pantiliners.

Try Peep Pantiliners for Girls and Peep Pantiliners for Women.

You are strong. No matter what accidentally spills out of your downstairs.

EMPOWERMENT EXERCISE: EMBODY A MAN

One of the best ways to feel empowered as a woman is to feel like a man. Men—especially your boss, Ted—are born with the feeling that they can do anything if they try. This is true for women too—just as long as you try harder! We can learn a lot from Ted about how to be a strong woman in the workplace, because, after all, a strong woman is just a man who gets called a "bitch" by Ted a lot more.

To enjoy the benefits of being a man, you need to *channel your inner man.* Specifically, channel your boss, Ted, the kind of inner man who doesn't let an opportunity to speak

his mind pass him by. Ted's got a charisma that makes deals happen. Ted gives unsolicited back rubs to his entire team. Ted's got a huge inner dick directing his tremendous inner manhood inside your tender inner womanhood. Here's how to embody your inner Ted.

Ted talks.

The best way to talk so others will listen is to talk like Ted—do a TED talk (yes, he changed his legal name to the all-capital

TED). Empower yourself by treating what you're saying as new and profound, even if it's just the sandwich options for the work lunch you're ordering for the office. Hold for applause after a particularly poignant insight. Get louder with each successive point you're making, lending it an important tone that says, "You're smarter for hearing what I have to say." Soon, you'll start to believe it is, just like Ted! How empowered is he?

Ted teaches.

Ted understands that it's his solemn duty to teach others everything he knows. Take a moment to summon the sleeping Ted inside you and let him educate your coworkers on the value of commitment and the merits and faults of Sriracha. That's why he always gets the raises he asks for! Remember, *Ted is inside you.*

Ted disrupts.

As your inner man, Ted isn't afraid to ruffle a few feathers. "Disrupting" other people, businesses, and economies may seem like a dick move, but is there any other way for a woman to get the job done? Ted isn't afraid to disrupt his own daughter's birth to take a work call, and neither should you. Can you do that? Can you empower yourself during the birth of your own daughter?

Ted pets heads.

One way of asserting your size is to remind others they are smaller than you. When you catch them in a vulnerable position, like sitting at their desk, empower yourself by walking over and petting them on the head or giving them a vigorous shoulder rub. Showing them they're doing a good job will let them know that you are doing an even better job. Because you are. Let's hear it for empowerment!

Ted pees standing up.

Your inner Ted pees standing up, because he's a man. Don't be afraid to hit the urinal and take up small talk with your fellow executives across the urinal. Where do you think all of the deals really happen? Where do you think they siphon their power from?

Remember, you can't feel empowered unless you act like a man, specifically Ted. Good luck, and don't ask any questions!

COMBATING WORKPLACE MISOGYNY WITH BODY CAMS

Overt sexual harassment in the workplace is difficult to ignore. But subtle sexism is more prevalent and even harder to report. Without hard evidence, it's nearly impossible to prove the existence of the "microaggressions" that occur on a daily basis. Thankfully, we've found a solution to both, with SafeWoman Mammocams™. We brought these patented sexism-seeking body cams into one office to root out the systemic misogyny in the workplace. Here's what happened.

Jean* was our first participant in the project, and workplace sexism reared its ugly head within hours after she put on the Mammocam. Jean was in a meeting when her boss,

Here is Jean with her low-profile MammoCam™.

---

* Names have been changed to protect the innocent.

Frank, asked her to take notes, leaving her male colleagues of equal rank able to participate freely in a brainstorming session unencumbered by such a menial task. When Jean asked if someone else might take notes this week, all the men told her she "was better at it" and "had neat handwriting." We confronted Frank with the footage a day later. His response was enlightening.

"Yes, I asked her to do that. I don't see the problem. Why are you here? This camera-bra getup is distracting. Did anyone approve this?"

Tory,* our second subject, also encountered the subtle office misogyny so familiar to us when she entered the office kitchen Tuesday. Her supervisor, Jim, remarked that all the milk and half-and-half had gone bad and "maybe she could pick some up on her lunch break." Tory explained to us that although she is not Jim's assistant, this was not the first time he'd made such a request. When we pressed Jim on the incident, he tried to deflect our scrutiny.

"So . . . did she pick up some milk? That stuff smelled funky. And why was she wearing those cameras on her . . . her chest? Why does there have to be two of them? Who are you guys?"

Later in the week, we went undercover with Marie, who, upon e-mailing her male colleague Tim to tell him that she'd found a serious flaw in a proposed project budget turned in by another colleague, Hasim, received a response from Tim telling her to "try to be a team player" and that people sometimes "found her tone grating." The bra footage of Marie reading this e-mail came as a shock to Tim.

"What is this? Is Marie being put on probation or something? Why are all the women wearing this camera bra? Couldn't she have done this with a regular camera? Are we doing product testing now?"

There you have it. Thanks to covert surveillance, subtle workplace sexism has been rooted out, and the offenders have been brought to light and made to face their transgressions. With SafeWoman Mammocams™ the perpetrators of *micro*-aggressions can finally face *major* consequences.

---

* This is a cool businesslike name we made up, isn't it? We're pretty good at this.

HOW TO DO MORE WITH 23 CENTS LESS

According to a *Huffington Post* article you saw once, women are paid on average 23 cents less than men for equal work.* Say whaaaat? There's nothing fair about institutionalized unfairness. However, as you should know by now, being a feminist means not letting institutionalized unfairness hold you back! It's also super important to not be seen as pushy while pushing back—feminists have worked hard to maintain a fun, likable public image! If you're not the "fighting for what's rightfully yours" kind of girl, here's how to get equal pay the passive way: by finding clever and creative ways to spend less and earn more!

Get married!

Hello, tax breaks! The sneakiest way to get paid the same as a man is to legally bind yourself to one. You'll be like Robin Hood, stealing from the rich and giving to the poor (you). If you're worried this isn't the most feminist fix, just think of it as a *fiscal* protest. Having a joint checking account is basically the same as burning a bra!

Stop eating dinners out—or in!

Eliminating one meal a day will not only get you closer to your financial goals; it'll also get you closer to your goal weight! You'll also save time by not doing all that cooking, grocery shopping, ordering at a counter, looking at a menu, chewing, tasting, swallowing, and pooping before bed. You're that much closer to earning the same as Todd, your boss's cousin who just got hired and can barely read!

Use one fewer tampon every period.

Little expenses add up! If you're wondering where the hole in your budget is, the answer might be in the hole in your crotch. Brand-name tampons can cost up to $12 for a box of forty, which is $16 in woman dollars. Yikes! Instead of cutting back on quality or buying generic,** simply use one fewer tampon each period. That saves $0.30 a month, which is $3.60 a year. That's $4.80 woman dollars to spend on anything you want!

---

* And that's not even accounting for the time we spend doing our "professional but young but respectable but fuckable" makeup every morning.

** Your vagina knows when you're being cheap and might retaliate by making you think of Mr. Rogers during sex.

Become your own boss (in addition to your regular boss)!

Maybe the corporate work-o-sphere just isn't cutting it. If you want to make up for the gaps in your paycheck, consider moonlighting as a sales rep for a cosmetics, skin-care, Tupperware, health-supplement, or knife company. All you have to do is front a few hundred bucks to get your starter kit, and the rest is a party! Your friends already buy products. Why not have them buy them from you? Remember, if you don't turn a profit and actually lose money on this deal, you probably didn't connect with enough high-school friends on Facebook and LinkedIn to "catch up" and tell them about this great opportunity to score an incredible deal.

Get a loose-change barrel.

You're gonna need a bigger jar! An empty sauce jar is not gonna hold a year's worth of lost wages, so head down to your sundries store and see if they'll part with one of the barrels they use to display old-timey candy. At the end of each day, empty out your pockets and purse of any loose change you have. After a few years, you should have a nice cushion in case you get fired for being "too go-getting."

~~Download a budget app~~ Downgrade your smartphone.

A flip phone has everything you need to slowly send texts, make phone calls, and even tell what time it is! Sure, a smartphone is considered a de facto necessary tool for keeping up in this modern workplace, but when you're earning only 77 cents on the dollar, you have to make up the difference somehow! Ask the fine folks at Metro PCS to dig deep in the backroom for a basic model that costs less per month than most Forever 21 rompers. You love a vintage find!

Simplify your living space.

As you learned that one time you got bedbugs, your car's backseat is the perfect size for sleeping! Living in an apartment can be costly, especially if you live in a major city. Plus, it's full of closets, kitchens, hallways, and other areas not meant for sleeping, so why pay for all that? Cut ties with that dead weight, sell or sublet it to some rube, and take to the open road. You can shower at your gym!* Finally, the fact that you sleep in a fetal position due to work-related stress nightmares will pay off.

---

* You're obviously not getting rid of your gym membership—that's a little extreme!

Start busking.

You still have that ukulele you bought back when you had bangs, so why not make it work for you? Let the world hear your take on "Somewhere over the Rainbow," and you might just see a pot of gold—or at least a tiny cup with two dimes and three pennies!*

You deserve to get paid equally, but in the meantime you gotta learn how to live with less. So readjust that budget, girl! You're so agreeable!

Try our feminist fortune-teller.

Getting bogged down by all these life decisions? Starting your career is hard, especially when people still treat you like a little girl. Remember when that was a good thing? Now, when you're feeling powerless in your profession and wondering what the future holds, cut out and use this feminist "Cootie Catcher" to find out where your career is headed.

Fold along the dotted lines, slide thumbs and forefingers under the squares, and move the fortune-teller back and forth to find your feminist professional future.

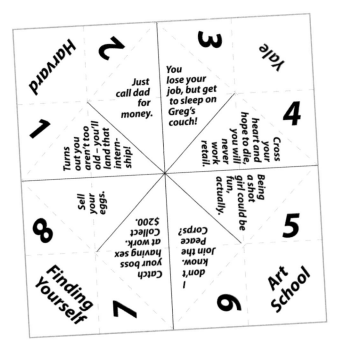

---

* That's 23 cents!

Feature: **A NOTE FROM RUTH BADER GINSBURG AFTER SHE'S HAD HER WINE**

H'you guys. What's shakin'?

I vowed this year to just have sparkling water—to stay away from the wine—but here I am, with a nice glass of wine, and I'm enjoying it, all right? I'm Ruth Bader Ginsburg, and I'm here to talk about my experience with sexism in the workplace over the years. WhileI've had the privilege of working with some of the greatest leaders and thinkers in the world, I've also faced challenges common to many women, like being called a "bossy" by Supreme Court Justice Roberts or having the entire Russian Federation tell me to "smile more." Ugh. Menss.

When I was starting out in 1960, I was denied a coveted clerk position for the Supreme Court because I was a woman, even though I had a recommendation from the dean of Harvard Law School. And when they told me I didn't get the job, I was patted on the head and told I was "probably bad at math."

So if you're wondering why I'm enjoying a glass offwine right now, it's because it's delicious. Do you want some? There's abox in the fridge.

I think it's our duty as women to fight for equality in the workkplace, because men can have a blind spot for woms's issues. Like sometimes when I was out dining with Justice Scalia, I was like, "Tonyy, do you even *know* what it's like to have a child?" And he seriously couldn't answer the question. You know why? It's because he couldn't. *He fucking couldn't.* RIP Tony.

One time a senator asked me if I had help writing my dissent for the Hobby Lobby decision. Yeah right! I said him that. "*Yeah right!*" Ha ha. I didntbut I wantdd to.

Nowadays I just keep telling myself, "Ruth, lay off the bottle of Barbera, you cando this when you get home." But you know what? I'm Ruth Bader Ginsburg. Are you srisly going to argue with me? I've gotten three honororororary doctorate of law degrees, but I still get asked to make coffee during oral arguments. Am I gonna be getting people coffee til'

(continued)

I'm ninety or will there be another woman to take over by then? "Don't jinx it, RBG," I say tomyself. "There's plenty of room for more women here." Do you realize how little space I take up in this chair?

I played Twsister once with SoonyB ono.

In the 1970s, I cofounded the first law journal devoted to women's rights, the Women's Rights Project at the ACLU, and helped extend the Equal Protection Clause to women for the first time. And mostof that time, Tony Scalia kept mistaking me for the receptionist and expecting me to order his birthday cake.

So inotherwords it's amazazing to see how far we've come from when I was just starting out in my career.

Now if you don't mind I think I'm going to close my eyes for just a b. . . .

Plinky Works Her Magic

An eye of a newt, and a leg of a toad,
That's all that you'll need to carry that load!
You work and you mother and have sex with
    Steve:
You're the witch-queen of Having-It-All
    Hallows' Eve!
Are you feminist now? Not yet, I believe!
Tut tut, titch titch,
Read on, bo$$ bitch!
Carjacking is easier than you think.

 DISCLAIMER

We're actually worried she might be telling the truth about some of these. Maybe just ignore her at this point.

HOW TO LOVE AND SEX

A FEMINIST INVOCATION OF

Lena Dunham

Adam.
Adam?
Adam!

Fine.
I'll get mine.
And his. And him. And him.

Feminist body.
Feminist sex.
It's in my writing.
I'm Sexipus Rex.

I am the star
Of my own sexual fantasy.
In the bedroom, I have agency.

Watch me eat.
Watch me pee.
Watch me eating while I pee.

Society will learn to love me.
Small-breasted feminist,
But filled with D.

SAINT LENA

PATRON SAINT OF HOOKUPS

IS DATING A MAN FEMINIST?

From the moment we were little girl babies, C-sectioned out of our mothers' flawless wombs, we have been conditioned to do everything in our power to Find A Man (FAM). But so much has changed since April of 1990! The Olsen twins have stopped singing about their brother and started dating much older men, literally nobody uses a Skip-It anymore (not even at Burning Man), and most important, *you no longer have to marry a man to have value in society.*

Now that you're almost feminist, you'll have many questions about how feminism applies to dating. Is dating a man feminist? Does feminism affect what I do in the bedroom? Does what I do in the bedroom affect feminism? Should feminism be giving me orgasms?[*] The answer is a resounding "Yes!" to all of these!

But the details of dating while feminist are much more complicated. Obviously, we don't *need* a man to be happy in life. Still, every woman has the right to honor her own desires, and if you *do* want a man, it's fine! Rest assured, *you can date a man and still be feminist!* But there is only one way to do so, and that's to *keep things equal.* Let us break your feminist dating concerns down to a few key points that are easy to digest, even on your first day off the Master Cleanse.

So how is dating a man feminist?

Whoa, good question! As far as we know, feminists throughout history have participated in the dating scene. You can be feminist and attached or feminist and looking to mingle. If you're having sex right now, don't stop! You can still be feminist! And more important, you can still have sex.

While there's no harm in dating, the crazy things we've done to FAM (Find A Man) in the past have gotten us into some real trouble and compromised our feminist standards. It's not entirely our fault; all the old-timey magazines of our youth taught us to hate our bodies and change ourselves to please a man. No way, patriarchy! We are powerful women who need to love ourselves before we can love another person. Listen up, ladies: if you have not yet learned to love yourself, *do not date.*[**] But once you're ready, just remember to . . .

---

[*] If you are being feminist enough, it should be giving you orgasms. Don't seek it out; it will come to you when it's ready.

[**] If you date without self-love, you run the risk of becoming the Sad Friend, and that is decidedly *not feminist* and also *incredibly depressing*. Look to your left and to your right. If there is no Sad Friend in your friend group, you are the Sad Friend!

Choose the dick before the dick chooses you.

Lena Dunham and Taylor Swift have taught us that, no matter how romantically adventurous you are, you need to try 'em all,* so make sure to get a good sampling of dick so you know what you want. Feminist dating is no longer about your being one of his options; it's about his being one of your options—one of many, *many* options.

Date a ton of people. Date until you don't enjoy it anymore. Date until you can't tell them apart from each other. The best way to find The One is to date so many Ones that you care a little bit less about which One you'll wed. So before you settle down and move in together, make sure you've explored Tinder for a few years, or at least until you start swiping right on your cousins.

Dating chill dudes vs. male feminists.

This is a chill dude.

This is a male feminist.

The next thing you need to know about feminism is that *the personal is political* and that, politically/personally speaking, it matters who you date. Even if nobody ever actually meets him, everything you do together has a chance of ruining feminism for everyone. This is why you basically have two options when it comes to feminist dating.

The first choice is the *chill dude.* If a dude is chill, he's usually not going to say something disrespectful, because he doesn't need to talk all the time like some other dudes. This *basically*

---

* In Taylor's case, she's sampling on more of an emotional level. Love U, Tay!

makes him feminist.* Chill dudes don't say dumb things about women because they're too busy waxing their vintage motorcycle, practicing Hacky Sack tricks, and laying down that D in an exceptionally chill way. You may never find out what he's thinking, but even if he did say something antifeminist, he's chill enough to remind you, "Just chill out already, okay?"

Your second option is a hot *male feminist.* You can usually find a male feminist yelling his progressive opinions loud enough for you to hear across the bookstore.** It's not very chill, but it is definitely feminist. A male feminist is brave and also very dateable, because he is using his male privilege to work for *your rights.* He could be doing *so many other things* with his male privilege—owning large boats, bulldozing the rain forest, getting into documentary filmmaking . . . you name it! But instead of fighting for his own personal gain, he chooses to fight for *you* by attempting to explain feminism better than you. He deserves so many feminist blow jobs for doing this! He may not be showing it, but he really wants that blow job. Seriously though! He didn't say anything to us, we swear!*** Which leads us to . . .

Oral is mutual.

All feminists give and receive oral in exact fifty-fifty proportions. It doesn't matter if he likes giving it more or vice versa; we've entered a new era of equality and the records must reflect that.

In this way, sex is actually a lot like voting. First you have to choose a candidate, then you go into a private place, and then you post a selfie afterward to show everyone what you just did! There's no wrong way to vote, but one candidate is probably better than the other, and everyone is kind of going to judge you for your choice. Also, having sex in a voting booth is super hot so we totally recommend that you try it! Rock the voting booth—literally!

In short, having sex with a man can still be feminist, as long as you sex the right kind of guy and have the right kind of sex with him. Come on, ladies, we're not burning bras and growing armpit hair here! We're just forcing you to choose the specific partners and activities that best reflect the values of feminism. And hey, you still get to do sex stuff!****

What's just as important as who you do that sex stuff with is who you *don't* do sex stuff with. Which brings us to . . .

---

* For a guy, at least.
** This is his mating call.
*** He's a good feminist. Come on, give him the blow job.
**** You *love* sex stuff!

HOW TO PUT DOWN THAT PICKUP ARTIST: MEET MISS NO, THE PROFESSIONAL PUT-DOWN ARTIST

You've all heard of pickup artists: goatee-having, sunglasses-wearing, fedora-doffing semiprofessional poker players who teach each other how to fuck *any* woman, despite hating all of them. They claim we can be won over by a simple combination of physical touch, mind games, and magic words. Sounds awful, right? Well, fear not. There is one woman who's out there fighting the good fight, every night.

Meet Miss No, the put-down artist.

PICKUP LINE: Have we met?

PUT-DOWN LINE: Perhaps. I used to volunteer in a shelter for hopeless dumbfucks.

MISS NO'S TAKE: This line has kept men away from me since college! Guys hate being called dumbfucks.

A former unemployment judge, Miss No (born Mona Lovegood-Hore) went pro a few years ago. She met us in a downtown sports bar recently, wearing black slacks, black platform sandals, and a medical ID bracelet that says, "Nice Try!" The natural brunette holds the Guinness World Record for most pickup lines shot down in a single late-night happy hour. She now teaches seminars across the country to help women learn the subtle art of convincing men to no longer want to pick them up. However, she wasn't always an expert on making boners disappear.

PICKUP LINE: Are you tired? Because you've been running through my mind all day.

PUT-DOWN LINE: Nope. It was a pretty short run. Do you get it? I'm calling you dumb. Also I'm in fantastic physical shape. Eat my dust, shitbug!

MISS NO'S TAKE: Can't emphasize this enough: call him dumb. Guys hate that. Also, guys like you to be fit, but they don't want you to be more athletic than they are. They hate that too!

Miss No got into the "not if you were the last man on earth" game organically. "I was just a regular girl, going to bars with my girlfriends, hanging at happy hour, just trying to get my party on," she tells us over a glass of water. "I was sick of all these red-faced investment bankers hitting on me with those pickup-artist techniques, like I was a piece of meat who could be controlled," she says. "So I started saying quippy things whenever they'd talk to me."

PICKUP LINE: Where have you been all my life?

PUT-DOWN LINE: I have been studying hard, working harder, and living fearlessly as a role model to the young girls in my community. Go fuck your own dick!

MISS NO'S TAKE: There's nothing less fuckable than a woman who uses words like "fearlessly" and "role model." Plus, it's considered rude to tell someone to fuck their own dick. He'll be flaccid before you know it!

At first she'd use simple rebuffs like "Fuck off" or "Not a chance." But Miss No tells us, "Once I was a few months in and really knew I was good at keeping men away, I started using puns and other creative wordplay. Then I straight-up called them dumb. And then a year in, I added the slam-poetry inflection. My friends started to notice and said I should share my secrets, and the rest is history."

PICKUP LINE: Come here often?

PUT-DOWN LINE: No. I only come at home, with my large vibrator. It was a gift from my older European paramour. We have a financial domination agreement that benefits both of us sexually. You are dumb!

MISS NO'S TAKE: Cocky young frat boys hate the idea of older foreign men with atypical sexual preferences.

Clearly she's doing something right! Smiling, she says, "I can proudly tell you that I have never had sex. Not even once." Wow! Miss No's got the info you need to know! Here's how she put down another pickup line.

PICKUP LINE: It seems like they're going to ask you to leave soon. . . . You're making all the other girls look bad.

PUT-DOWN LINE: Sir, you are wrong. I lift up other women. I live for my sisters. I'd die for them. If leave I must, leave I will. Long live the matriarchy! Your tiny dick is dumb!

MISS NO'S TAKE: His dick might actually fall off. I've seen it happen a few times. I love my work!

Some put-down tips to try at home.

Miss No's methods are great for women who live out loud, but are a *little* extreme for amateur boner rejecters. Like the girl on the right side of the instructor in a workout video, we've tweaked Miss No's tips for lower-impact everyday use. Here are some great strained and awkward things to say while praying his dick goes away.

PICKUP LINE: Have we met?

PUT-DOWN LINE: Umm maybe? Ha . . .

OUR TAKE: Guys like when you're nice! Just make sure you're not too nice, so he knows you're not into it. Not sure how to strike that balance? Better stay home until you figure it out!

PICKUP LINE: Are you tired? Because you've been running through my mind all day.

PUT-DOWN LINE: Ha ha, whaaat? Ha ha . . . Umm, no, ha ha . . . Hi . . .

OUR TAKE: Play along and show him you can laugh! Also, awkwardly saying hello because you don't know what else to say will come across as quirky—the most alluring of all female awkwardness! You can weasel your way out of sleeping with him later on, when several of your friends have to drag you into a taxi to keep you away from him.

PICKUP LINE: Where have you been all my life?

PUT-DOWN LINE: Ohio . . .

OUR TAKE: Go ahead, answer his question! Guys like that. Hopefully he'll leave you alone, but not because you were too pushy; he just saw some other girl with blonder hair. Good luck, Ohio!

PICKUP LINE: Come here often?

PUT-DOWN LINE: Yeah! About once a week. You? (whisper) But, um, I have a boyfriend so . . .

OUR TAKE: Make sure you're not rude and answer him with an approximation of how often you come to this bar. It's important to make sure he knows you have a boyfriend, but telling him might hurt his feelings. Split the difference between saying something and not saying something by whispering it. He might just hear your boundary and not cross it!

PICKUP LINE: It seems like they're going to ask you to leave soon. . . . You're making all the other girls look bad.

PUT-DOWN LINE: Ha ha, oh no!

OUR TAKE: Be afraid! It makes you look super thin.

So there you have it: the best unfuckable put-down tips that work every time and also some more polite ones that won't work. Use these at your next pub night to be seen as either frigid and bitchy or pushover prey. TGIF!

FEMINIST FIRST DATES

As feminists, we reclaim epithets, wood, and vintage clothing, so why wouldn't we reclaim dating too? On a truly feminist date, there are no rules—except that every part of it must be precisely fair and mathematically equal. You want to make it clear that you have no interest in depending on a man for *anything*. Not even his money. *Not even his HBO GO password.*[*]

Crafting a feminist first date takes a little extra effort, but you know what? So does foraging for a man who cherishes you as a human being of equal or greater value. Whether you manifested him with your own divine energy or found him on Bumble, honor that effort by setting a date that is a fair exchange of ideas, rituals, fluids, and money. You might be the fairest of them all, but that doesn't mean that your first date shouldn't be *even fairer*. Dating is about equality now.

Because this date is going to set the tone for the rest of your relationship, you need to be firm and consistent in doling out chiv-*her*-lry throughout your time together. You need to show him that you don't *need* a man; you would just *prefer* to have one around in the most equitable way possible. Here are some key things to keep in mind to make sure your first date is equal as fuck.

A firm handshake shows him you have neither the upper nor the lower hand on this date.

---

[*] At least until things get serious.

Start with a firm handshake.

Nothing sets the tone of an equal date like a firm handshake to let him know you're both on an equal playing field. Give it a firm grip that says, "I could probably beat you at arm wrestling, but that's not what this date is about." Nobody's gonna gain the upper hand on *this* date.

Walk through doors at the same time.

Save the sad, basic chivalry for your second date. Avoid the never-ending "After you" exchange by agreeing to walk through all doorways at exactly the same time.* This will require you to enter all rooms sideways and close together, which should make up for the lack of intimacy in that first handshake.

Drink the same amount.

Don't go letting him drink more 'cause he's a "man" or letting him get you drunk 'cause you're a "woman." Look him square in the eye and go drink for drink or shot for shot with him, if it's that kind of date. Oh, it is? Okay, good. It's time to get this shit *started.*

Order the same entrée for dinner.

It should be the second-most expensive thing on the menu,** and you should eat it all. *Don't let him get ahead of you. Never let him get ahead.* Susan B. Anthony is dead, and she is *watching* you.

Offer to split the check, spill your purse everywhere, and then say, "We have to figure out tip togetherrr!"

Fuck it, you're drunk. This is equal as fuck! Tip the waiter your iPhones. #Equal.

---

* No matter how narrow. Do you want to win at feminism or not?
** You're allergic to the first.

Go in for the kiss at exactly the same time.

Fucking *go for it!* You're already fuckin' drunk. Why not match his move with an equal and opposite move? *Nobody goes first on this date. Nobody.*

Have mutual simultaneous oral sex.

Oh, it's a fuckin' mess going on down there. This shit is getting sloppy. Just keep it equal. Oh I'm sorry, does equality "not feel good" or "feel kinda weird"? Too fucking bad. Keep at it, unless the idea of living in a feudal patriarchal wife-selling society sounds *good.*

If he squirts, you squirt.

This is what all the drinking was for. *Don't hold back!! Take what is yours!*

HOW TO STICK WITH THE DATING APPS YOU HATE

Being a woman on the Internet is like being a celebrity, but without the money or the free shoes. You're constantly trying to politely decline your suitors without making them feel alienated or encouraging them to follow through with their death threats. Except you have to do this without a PR team or even a celebrity girl gang.* The horror!

We all know online dating is even harder, especially on shallow dating apps like Tinder. It may make you want to give up when dudes only message you looking for a gross, rushed hookup at 3 A.M. But we feminists don't give up. Like cream (but with less saturated fat), we rise to the top, even in misogynistic environments. *Rising above it all* is a skill that every feminist must learn, and we can do it by totally *owning* misogynists, one text at a time.

There are a lot of ways to flip the script and totally *own* it in online dating, so the next time a dude tries to order you up like bacon,** you know how to make *him* feel like the juicy piece of meat that *you* get to turn over.

---

* We don't know who said the Internet makes your life easier, but it probably was a man!

** It's called Tinder because men are trying to start a fire to cook us alive.

Make the first move.

One way to put guys back on the defensive is to objectify them before they objectify you. So instead of being forced to respond to a message from a match like this one:

You can message him first with:

Give him a taste of his own medicine.

The next time you get an opening line that makes you feel lesser-than, flip that script and show him what it's like to get it right back:

Make all your matches seem like accidents.

If a dude does get around to messaging you first, message him:

Message him something nonsensical.

Another way to throw a guy off his game and show him that you can't even be bothered to form sentences for him is to message him something short that literally makes no sense. He'll probably wonder if he isn't getting the new Internet slang or if you're insulting him:

Here are a few more tips that take a few notes from *his* playbook.

Put only job-related accomplishments in your bio.

Don't talk about whether you're looking for a relationship. Instead, list your career achievements, special skills, and salary. He'll see that you're more than just a pretty face for him to come onto.*

Be surrounded by hot dudes in your pic.

Wanna make the guys feel inadequate right off the bat? Have armfuls of buff men in your photos. Even if he matches with you and messages you for a hookup, he'll know that he means just as little to you as you do to him.

---

* Assuming he reads any of your profile.

Never match anyone.

Wanna play hardball? Swipe left on all of them. Every single one. They may have forgotten your profile the second they swiped whatever on you, but you'll know. And they'll never have the satisfaction of matching with you.

Above all, remember it's important that you keep using this terrible app, no matter what. Having lots of bad dating experiences is the only way to find the one bad dating experience you want to stick with for the rest of your life. Happy swiping!!

Special "Dan Only" Feature

Whether you're spying on one particular Dan or only end up dating guys named Dan, our patented Dan-Only button makes finding Dans a breeze. Tap it and watch your matches get whittled down to just the good stuff: the Dans! They're good listeners, they get along with your cat, and their penises are fine. This filter is only available for paid premium subscribers, along with other helpful features like Height Verification, Expert Fingerers Club, and the "No Brians" button. So easy!

Men Cannot Respond

Let's face it: relationships are a waste of time. Femdr believes that the best date is one that never happens. Not only will you avoid his gross-ass pickup lines and self-important humblebrags; you'll also avoid all the agony that comes with romantic entanglements. Although many of you may feel frustrated by this feature on an otherwise promising dating app, remember that you said you would focus on yourself this year. And now if guys really want to get your attention, they have to do it the romantic way, by running down the street in the rain with their shirt open.

Femdr

For feminists who want to date but can't!

HOW TO GET CATCALLED FOR YOUR *PERSONALITY*

Catcalling: *n.* Getting judged by strange men IRL instead of online, like you normally do.

One of the biggest issues that women face today is catcalling and street harassment. And just like your Instagram stalker, catcallers only seem to care about your looks. You're a beautiful woman on the inside and out, and you deserve to be yelled at about *all* your beauty, especially the beauty that's inside of you.* Getting catcalled for your personality, not just your looks—*that's* what feminism is fighting for!

Our mothers and grandmothers may have welcomed unsolicited comments from men in the past, but we now know that street harassment objectifies and dehumanizes female bodies. We deserve better than what our foremothers merely tolerated. Also no offense, but Grandma didn't know shit about feminism (rest in peace, Grandma; it's not your fault!!).

Here's how to get catcalled for your personality.

Work on your personality.

You're a woman, so face it: you can't be a fly on the wall. You should expect to be targeted on the street by a man who says he wants to crawl inside your sweatpants. But if you want him to yell out something more interesting, start the conversation for him by *being* interesting. Maybe it's time to pick up a hobby? Try reading *The New Yorker* or *The Economist* if you want to impress your catcaller. He'll be sure to tell you that you look *smart* in that cute little outfit of yours.

---

* In your brain or your heart or wherever.

Yell a lot.

It seems pretty easy, but girls who yell a lot typically have a "loud" personality.* If you want to take the focus off of your boobs and onto your *words,* you should scream those words. Guys will be like, "Damn, she's really hot *and* loud!"

Join Greenpeace.

One awesome way to make guys not focus on your looks is to wear a T-shirt that says "Greenpeace" and then ask them for money. When you make the first move, guys will be compelled to say things like, "Sorry," "No," and "Fuck off, you dumb bitch," instead of the usual jabs about your body. At least you know he's rejecting you for something you really believe in!

Be kind.

If you happen to see a perfectly nice homeless person standing right next to your future cat-caller, go above and beyond to help that person in need. Share your meal with her, give her some money or the name of a shelter, and you'll have your catcaller saying, "Damn, girl, you really went above and beyond in helping the less fortunate. You know who else you could help with that ass who's less fortunate—*me*!"

Make a joke!

Guys don't just want a pretty face; they want a girl with a sense of humor! If a catcaller starts making blow-job noises as you walk by him, say something clever like, "You got something stuck in your throat?" After he stops the sucking noises, he'll be like, "That bitch can take it *and* give it right back!" Any guy who can't appreciate a girl who can make him laugh shouldn't be catcalling in the first place.

There are plenty more feminist ways to get strangers to compliment you on your kindness, and if you followed our first directive above, you should be on your way to your own ideas as well!

---

* Remember Debra??

It's not enough to remain vigilant in this modern, rape-filled world.

Made by men, for women, to attack men, the Vagilante is the only self-defense multi-tool you'll need to prevent the dozen types of rape the world can throw at you on a nightly basis.

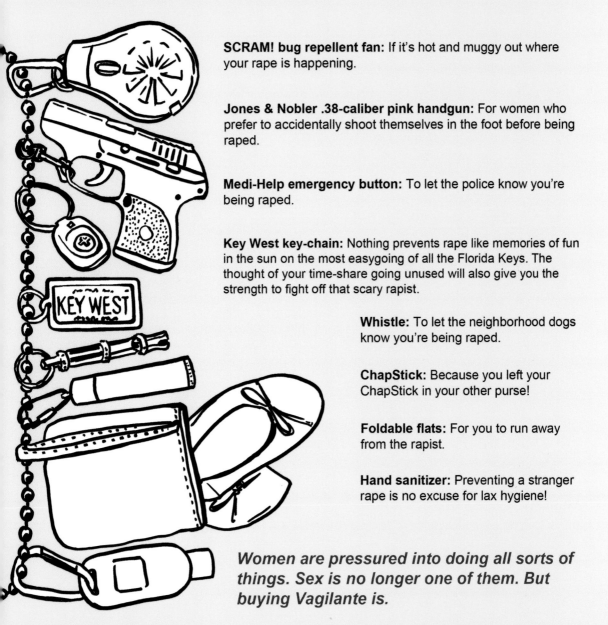

SCRAM! bug repellent fan: If it's hot and muggy out where your rape is happening.

Jones & Nobler .38-caliber pink handgun: For women who prefer to accidentally shoot themselves in the foot before being raped.

Medi-Help emergency button: To let the police know you're being raped.

Key West key-chain: Nothing prevents rape like memories of fun in the sun on the most easygoing of all the Florida Keys. The thought of your time-share going unused will also give you the strength to fight off that scary rapist.

Whistle: To let the neighborhood dogs know you're being raped.

ChapStick: Because you left your ChapStick in your other purse!

Foldable flats: For you to run away from the rapist.

Hand sanitizer: Preventing a stranger rape is no excuse for lax hygiene!

Women are pressured into doing all sorts of things. Sex is no longer one of them. But buying Vagilante is.

IS YOUR GUY FEMINIST?

Now that you're exploring your feminist identity, you may find yourself looking at your man in a different way, wondering if he's as woman-friendly as you are. If you can answer yes to the questions below, there's a good chance he's also feminist!

- Does he go down on you?
- Does he have longer hair?
- Does he have one or more sisters?
- Has he ever watched a movie you wanted to watch without complaining?
- Has he ever listened to one of your friends talk without calling her "mouthy"?
- Can he say any of the following names without scoffing?

    – Lena Dunham

    – Hillary Clinton

    – Rosie O'Donnell

    – His mom

    – Any woman who's ever displayed an opinion

    – Really, any woman

- When you have your period, does he not skip town?
- Did he not dump you when you cut your hair short?
- Did he not dump you when you took a dump?
- Does he wear glasses?
- Did he go to grad school for something involving books?
- Does he seem like he'd be the type of person who'd give mouth-to-mouth to an animal?
- Has he ever danced with an elderly woman at a wedding?
- When you say the phrase "Grand Theft Auto," does he cock his head to the side like he's confused?

If you said yes to any of these, your guy is *probably* feminist! Lucky you!

REBRANDING YOUR RELATIONSHIP ISSUES AS FEMINIST ISSUES

Now let's say you've found yourself a hunky male feminist to bone. First, congratulations! You have a man! Now, there's a critical question you need to ask yourself: Is my *relationship* feminist?

We've already confirmed that you can be a feminist while dating a man, but there are still lots of things about your relationship that can be backward, paternalistic, or just really annoying to people around you. As a good feminist, you want to avoid as many of those things as possible.

Remember, literally everything you do in life will affect your street cred as a feminist. Even the stuff you do in the bedroom, like pegging your boyfriend, or calling your mom after pegging your boyfriend. It's hard to be political all the time, but if you learn to find the feminist angle to things you already do, you'll find that almost anything can be feminist.*

If you're going to make all of your relationship issues feminist issues, you have to ask yourself the hard questions: What does your relationship stand for? Love? Equality? Calorie counts on *all* restaurant menus? The correct answer is: feminism. Here's how to reframe your existing relationship issues as feminist issues.

Cheating: Not Feminist

Oh, girl. Don't tell us he cheated already. This is not something you can allow in a feminist relationship, and you better deal with it. What? You're the one who cheated?**

Polyamory: Feminist!

Look, it sounds like you guys are into some freaky shit. Why not just put it out in the open and embrace polyamory! Polyamory is a consensual, open, honest, loving relationship involving more than two people. Make sure everybody knows your sexploits are *super* consensual and you're just in a really progressive relationship! You'll have people asking, "How do you juggle all that dick?"

---

* Exclusions: racism, football, steak.
** Hmm. We're gonna need more context.

Lack of Communication: Not Feminist

A lack of communication is not only unhealthy behavior for a serious relationship; it can lead to your stifling your own voice and not expressing your own wants and needs in a relationship, creating a serious imbalance with lasting negative effects.

A Ball Gag: Feminist!

There's no expectation to talk about your feelings when you have a ball gag in your mouth. And you two can trade off as you both *consensually* refuse to talk about your feelings. And it's kinky as hell, you little Christmas ham!

Cleaning Up After Him: Not Feminist

You're a busy working woman, and constantly cleaning up after your filthy, inconsiderate, mess-leaving boyfriend only encourages more bad behavior from him, and an increasingly unequal relationship.

A Power-Shifting Role-Play Where You Dress in a Sexy Maid Outfit and Clean While He Jerks Off: Feminist!

Recontextualize a traditional relationship structure with *this* power move! You'll be literally overflowing with sex positivity as you hump the couch arm and scrape the old Chinese food off the coffee table while he tells you to *scrape harder*. This gets you off. Nobody will question this as a feminist act.

And there you have it! Just some *slight changes* in your everyday relationship behavior can make you look and sound even more feminist than you already are. Don't forget to blog about it!

FEMINIST THINGS THAT WILL GET HIM OFF

Just because you're a feminist doesn't mean you can't give a man mind-blowing, dick-rocking, climax-filled sex. Contrary to popular belief, feminists are often *better* at sex than their non-feminist counterparts. That's because feminists aren't afraid to try new things, like taking a dominant role or putting a finger in his butt. Here's a list of feminist things that will get him hot and make him come so hard, it'll rattle the foundations of the patriarchy!

Not Wearing a Bra

Nothing's as feminist as letting your boobs fly free, liberated from the patriarchal confinement and restriction of a bra. Going bra-free also happens to be a great way to give your man a boner. Your breasts are a moving target that can't be ignored!

Freeing the Nipple

What's more feminist *and* more boner-inducing than not wearing a bra? Freeing the nipple in its entirety! The double standard that polices the visibility of women's bodies is an important issue that should be protested through militant half-nudity. Visible breasts are also known to arouse heterosexual men—a win-win for feminism!

Firm Consent

You know how feminists have sex? By consenting to it, vocally and enthusiastically. Giving firm consent shows a man you're feminist, while also turning him on. So go ahead and say, "Yeah, I wanna F you. I wanna F you so good." Then make him ask again, so you can consent even more firmly. You're a strong feminist, which he will respect—and so will his growing penis! Keep consenting until you both come at the same time.

Striptease!

Be his private dancer—for your benefit! With each strip, you'll be owning your curves and telling the world your female body is nothing to be ashamed of. Plus, it'll make his dick hard. Neat!

Pegging

Would a nonfeminist be so willing to dominate, take charge, and penetrate in the bedroom? Only if she were a man. Reverse the hegemonic power structures of the bedroom, while you also make him orgasm real big.

A Finger in His Butt

So maybe your guy's not ready for the full silicone-dick treatment. That doesn't mean you can't rectally pleasure him like a feminist. A strong woman isn't afraid to be the digital inserter, and a sensitive man isn't afraid to be the inserted-in. His butt and his penis will like that a lot.

There are so many ways to use feminism to get him off. So get to multitasking and fight for equality, all while maintaining that stiffy!

HOW TO BE SEX POSITIVE EVEN WHEN YOU'RE BLOATED

The contemporary feminist movement is all about sex positivity. Women enjoy and desire sex just as much as men, and we aren't afraid to say it! Since being sexually empowered is as important as being politically empowered, it's important you don't set the movement back by *not* wanting to have sex. Only problem is, you just ate a huge burrito. Here's how to be sex positive even when you're packing heat.

Remember, big is beautiful.

Don't let your swollen belly make you ashamed of your physical appearance. Your bloated-ness just means there's more to love! After all, this gas-filled stomach is just one more curve in your newly bloated, bodacious arsenal. So instead of saying, "I feel full," tell yourself, "I feel *beauty-full.*"

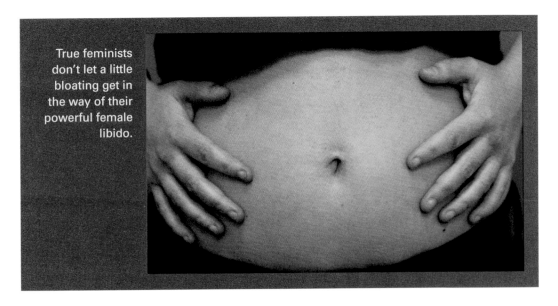

True feminists don't let a little bloating get in the way of their powerful female libido.

Pretend your farts are just lil' queefs.

Farts are not hot—but queefs are! After all, they come from your vagina, and vaginas are sexy 100 percent of the time. If you just envision your farts as queefs, you'll *feel* sexier even as that extra guac courses through your intestinal tract. *Feeling* sexy is *being* sexy, you beautiful woman!

Take some Gas-X and watch some porn!

Is the sexuality of your pelvic chakra being upstaged by problems in your root chakra? Sometimes a direct route is best. Pop an antigas pill, turn on some female-friendly porn, and let nature take its course. You'll be out of "too much food, feel bad" territory and back in "sex good" land before you know it!

Have a threesome.

Still feeling fat? Try having a threesome. It's sexually adventurous, and it'll take the focus off of you. Just try it!*

Go blonde.

There's something about being blonde and taking on a performed persona that gets some women feeling frisky. So don a wig or bleach it out. The new you is horny and gas-free!

Get boudoir photos taken.

It's time to feel sexually liberated and liberated from this abdominal cramping! Why not do it with the encouragement of a photographer who specializes in tasteful sexy photos? He (or she!) will help you embrace your sexuality to the extent that you barely notice your own debilitating lactose intolerance.

Remember, the first rule of feminism is sex positivity. The second rule is avoid dairy. The third rule is if you just had dairy, it's okay, we all slip up sometimes; just don't lose the sex-positivity thread. Now get it, girl!

---

* Just *try* it! Come on.

MEET ROY, THE HUNKY MALE FEMINIST

For all you ladies who think that a good feminist man is hard to find— we hope you brought an extra pair of panties for this one! Meet Roy, a graduate student in theater at Sarah Lawrence and the hunky male feminist of your dreams! Let's see what he has to say about the state of equality today and if he might be interested in you.

Roy loves women who break the mold.

Roy isn't weirded out when an athletic girl has a "mannish" body. "In fact, it's a huge turn-on," says Roy. "I think strong, powerful women are incredibly sexy," he adds. "And who needs boobs, anyway? Definitely not me."

Roy went to Vassar.

Roy, who majored in Women's and Gender Studies at Vassar College as an undergraduate, fearlessly contributed to class discussions with the same fervor as his female classmates. "Just thinking of everything that my sisters have gone through just gets me so worked up. Sometimes I need to go blow off steam afterward, like at the gym with the guys, or just chilling in the gym with the guys. But also, fuck the patriarchy, you know? Men are *such bitches*."

Roy loves consent.

Speaking of consent, Roy calls himself the "most consenting man alive." "Go ahead, Google me—literally no man asks for consent more than I do. I will look you in the eye and ask three times, 'Can I have sex with you?' She has to say yes all three times for us to proceed, and even then, I still won't do it, out of respect."

Roy also has a six-pack.

We won't argue with that!

Roy loves a woman's right to choose.

Roy believes in reproductive rights for all women and is fiercely devoted to defending a woman's right to choose. "Women who make decisions about their own bodies are really sexy," says Roy, while stretching on a ballet bar before dance rehearsal. "I'm primarily attracted to that political position."

Roy hates catcallers.

This hunky ex-gymnast and current dancer has also had countless talks with catcallers about their behavior. "Sometimes they need to hear it from a fellow guy. A beautiful woman deserves to be treated with respect. I just love my girls and want to treat them like queens. Some guys just don't appreciate the gift of female friendship."

Roy has cool tattoos.

He even has "Born This Way" tattooed on his lower back. Born *what* way, Roy? Ha ha ha, oh Roy!

Roy is a lover and a fighter—for women's dignity.

Roy is fighting on the front lines of "microaggressions" against women and consistently calls out other men for their bias. "Lots of guys don't even know they're doing it. I would almost feel bad for them, if it weren't for their constant refusal to check their own privilege." Roy, who identifies as "firmly straight" but feels "politically queer," adds, "It's my job to tell them. If I don't, who will?"

But the big question remains, would Roy date *you*? "I think all women are beautiful," said Roy, and then he asked us if he could see a pic of you first.

NOW, ABOUT YOUR LESBIAN PHASE . . .

Whether it's five seconds, five years, or your entire life, your lesbian phase is a beautiful part of the feminine experience. If you've ever been attracted to one of your girlfriends, it's totally okay! Everyone goes through a lesbian phase at some point.

When we went through our collective lesbian phase, some of us were afraid of what others would think. Others were brave and unapologetic in flaunting our new girlfriend around the office. And some others have continued the lesbian phase until this day. But the most important thing to know is that it's just a phase. A totally hot, brave phase. Our feminist mothers and sisters worked tirelessly to pave the path, so that today we can be with whoever we want to be if we're on a quick break from the D.

Thanks to feminism, female celebrities can hold hands in public without ruining their careers,* we can make out with a girl at a party to get attention from Brad, and Dana has the

HOW TO DO YOUR LESBIAN PHASE RIGHT: ELLEN

Back in 1997, Ellen DeGeneres was the first woman to ever come out. We'll never forget that day that she was on the cover of *Time* magazine, saying, "Yep, I'm going through my lesbian phase."

We admire Ellen's bravery for being the first woman to ever make this great leap, especially when there weren't any other lesbians in the world to have a lesbian phase with yet.** Fortunately, Ellen met her only natural counterpart in the world, Portia de Rossi, who is beautiful and also happened to be going through her lesbian phase at the same time. Portia and Ellen's lesbian phase has shown us that we can be hot *and* lesbian *and* have the love of moms all over the country. Who could have imagined *that* thirty years ago? Look at how far we've come!

---

* At least until they turn forty!

** If a woman has a lesbian phase and there's nobody there to watch, did she really have a lesbian phase?

right to touch your friend's boobs for a racy Instagram without fear of life imprisonment. *That's* gay rights. Thanks, Stonewall!

So did you meet a cute girl in Pilates and want to ask her out? Did you end up having strong feelings for her and express them by having sex? Have you spent the past five years living together with your adopted daughter and three dogs? Okay, that's kind of long, but it'll sure make for a juicy story to tell your girlfriends over brunch! No matter how long or short, here's a quick rundown on how to frame your lesbian phase (which is super brave of you, by the way!).

If your lesbian phase lasts five seconds to two minutes . . .

"It just reminded me how much I love dick."

This is the most common lesbian phase that women experience in college or right after a divorce. That's when you gotta let your freak flag fly! Whether it's an amorous glance or a passionate kiss, you've now internalized hundreds of years of struggle for gay rights and really understand what it's like to overcome the odds in a way that's *super hot*.

Now when you're talking with your girls about it over brunch, you can tell them, "It was super hot, but it just reminded me just how much I luh dat D!" Then you'll all raise your bottomless mimosas to the dick and get back to dickin' that dick.

If your lesbian phase lasts two minutes to two years . . .

"I just needed a break from all the dick."

Whether you've gotten out of a crappy relationship with a guy or never had a relationship with a guy at all because you're generally not attracted to them, you might find yourself in a lesbian relationship at some point. Right on! But this is also just a phase. A really beautiful phase. The best way to tell your girlfriends over brunch would be to say, "I just needed a break." Your girls understand that everybody needs a break sometimes, especially from dick that is very good. Too much good dick can ruin your ability to appreciate dick forever! Now get back on that *dee-yick*!

If your lesbian phase lasts two to five years . . .

"I thought she was the love of my life, but I guess I was wrong. Back to dick!"

Is there something you need to tell us? *Just kidding!* You're just in the "your love grows for her every time you look her in the face" phase of your lesbian phase. You might also be going through the phase of moving in and building a life together in a true partnership. Like most relationships, though, this one will probably hit some dicks in the road, and things might not work out. It's okay! So you thought she was the love of your life, but you just realized that her problems are representative of *all* women. Ha ha, am I right, ladies? We hate ourselves!! See you at brunch so we can talk about that big veiny *djee-yuukkkk*.

If your lesbian phase lasts five years to eternity—an eternal union . . .

"This shit will make a wild story when I'm dead (and finally back on dick)."

Whoa, that lesbian phase lasted longer than we all thought! Maybe you're destined to meet your future husband in the afterlife or another life altogether, if you believe in that kind of thing, 'cause that reincarnation dick is *nasty-good ghost dick*. We always knew you'd save the best for last!

LEZ-SPIRATION: STYLE INSPO FOR YOUR LESBIAN PHASE

Shave the side of your head.

This edgy haircut shows that you don't give a fuck, and you might be totally into chicks. Maybe not? Either way, it'll grow out eventually.

Wear a temporary "dyke" tattoo.

This is a great tattoo to show your pride for a very fixed amount of time. Reapply if necessary!

Read a super-dykey book like *Girl, Interrupted*.

It's super short and super dykey, and you'll finish it in a month. Like you, it's ambiguous enough to leave people on the train asking, "Is she or isn't she?"

PLANNING A FEMINIST WEDDING

Although the tradition of marriage reinforces the notion that a woman's worth is tied to a man, we also know weddings are so fucking gorgeous they make us cry. And we know we don't all *need* a big, beautiful wedding day; we all *deserve* one. Here's how to have a breathtakingly stunning wedding that doesn't overly reflect the patriarchal system of marriage.

Wear a different-colored wedding dress.

Order a custom wedding dress from Vera Wang, but instead of going the traditional route, ask her to make it out of peacock feathers dyed black, with a black diamond–encrusted bodice. People will be like, "That bride is so fucking gorge, it's making me question everything about traditional gender roles."

Make your maid of honor a guy.

If your maid of honor is your gay BFF, no one would mistake you for a future homemaker. Having your gaybie there to wipe tears out of your eyes* says, "I don't follow the rules—I don't even know how to turn on the vacuum cleaner."

Wear colorful heels.

Pops of color in your wedding let people know that you're having fun on your own terms and that you will never fully submit to a life under patriarchal rule, especially not one that involves touching raw meat. Make your own steak, hubby!

Have the groom wear shorts.

OMG, a man in a short pantsuit can look so, so fresh and adorable.** Also, putting him in shorts will give him a more boyish look that assures all your guests that *you* will be the one wearing the pants in this marriage, even if today you are wearing a dress.

---

* Agree upon duties such as these in advance. You do not want to be caught without a tear-wiper day of.
** But obvs, he gots to have the legs for it.

Wear a handmade tiara or crown.

One doesn't have many occasions to wear a beautiful headpiece, so go for it on your wedding day! This accessory also shows your man and the bridal party that you expect to be treated like a rustic farm kween—a.k.a., *not* a wifey!

Play fempowering music at the reception.

Anything that gets your girls dancing is fempowering. By playing only the most danceable hits, you'll show your friends that this marriage is all about your continuing to live life to your feminist fullest.

Don't toss the bouquet.

Tossing the bouquet implies that all your female guests want and need to get married as soon as possible. Not to mention tossing the bouquet is known to be a little tacky at this point. So just don't do it. Replace this tired tradition with something cuter, like giving the bouquet to the couple who've been married the longest. This isn't to imply that staying in a marriage for the long haul is inherently a good thing, since Grandma Jeanne probably couldn't leave Grandpa Bo even if she wanted to, due to societal pressures. It's just nice to be nice to old people!

Weddings make people crazy, and jealous friends and family will be rushing to judge you. By implementing these tips you won't give them the slightest reason to question your commitment to feminism on your big day. Now go and make your wedding a feminist one!

Plinky's Love Spell

Bibbity bobbity, single and straight,
Hocus and pocus and won't stay out late,
Respectful and sexful and kind-eyed and tall,
You've found him—the femin-est one of
     them all!
But it's not over just 'cause you're belle of
     the ball!

Kip kip, koop koop,
Read on now, you poop!

I have had sex with several war criminals.

⚠ DISCLAIMER

Okay cool, so this was a huge mistake. But hey, she's happy for you, right?

HOW TO SAVOR BEING A SAVIOR

Oprah

Believe it,
Achieve it,
It's The Secret.
But I won't keep it.

Mhmm.
Amen.
This book will make you whole again.

And this soy candle,
And this fleece robe.
From the flea market to the red carpet,
Swathed in Nate Berkus for Target.

Let's find our true selves with Gayle King.
Are you one of your Favorite Things?

Meditate.
Have some chai.
Go inside yourself and have a good cry.

And when we're through,
Let's look at inequality, and see what we can do.

You get a rebirth.
You get a rebirth.
You get a rebirth.
Let's feed the homeless, with these Le Creuset.
We're super souls, every day.

That's what I know for sure.

SAVING THE WORLD, SAVING OURSELVES

Being a feminist is exhausting; revitalize your feminist spirit while also finding time to save the world.

If you've made it this far, congrats—feminism is now your life's purpose! As we all know, your life's purpose is something you should prioritize above all else, so you need to go easy on yourself while you figure out how to pursue it. That means that while you're helping others you must also find time to treat yourself.

Treating yourself is one of the most important parts of being a woman. But it can be hard to say yes to that third glass of rosé without a pang of guilt over the people who are going without *any rosé at all*. This is the modern feminist dilemma. How can we devote our lives to equality and justice without letting it eat into our busy workweek? How do we foment a social revolution while also making time for self-care? How do we build a progressive utopia without missing Zumba and our after-Zumba wine?

No matter how day-drunk you are, it's hard to forget all the major problems plaguing our world. Women are still struggling for basic rights, poverty and injustice are rampant, and your social worker friend Brenna *still* can't afford eyelash extensions. Something's gotta change, and it's your job as a feminist to talk about changing it. But you can't do that without having your own spiritual transformation into a healthy, balanced woman. The third world doesn't want your second best, so put yourself first! It's that level of enlightenment that's going to help you help others on an Oprah-like scale.

THIS WOMAN donated her unused 20% off Bed Bath & Beyond coupons and gave them to women in need.

THIS WOMAN venmos orphans.

Fortunately, some of our favorite brands have made it easier than ever to ease our nagging guilt and help us help others. It's true: today you can treat yourself *and* save the world, *all at the same time*! Think it's impossible? Well, we never thought Skechers could make a sneaker that firms *and* tones while you walk, but who's laughing now?* All around the world, companies are putting their money where their mouth is by raising awareness about issues like body image, making commercials that show they care, manufacturing yoga pants that are more aware than other yoga pants, and donating yearlong supplies of facial tissues to impoverished children in developing countries.

The following suggestions will help you find your own way to make a difference in the world, while also leaving you plenty of time to feel #inspired, #blessed, and #totallywowed bytheuniverse.

You can't treat others unless you treat yourself first.

Before you even think about talking about doing something for someone else, it's important to ask yourself: "Have I practiced enough self-care to be ready to care for others?" Flight attendants have been telling you for years: you have to put your own oxygen mask on before trying to strap it on your terrified son. Have you ever tried inspiring underprivileged youth after getting less than seven hours of sleep? Trust us, it turns out *horribly*. You don't want to *un*inspire underprivileged youth, do you? If you're not in a relaxed, blissful mind-set, you'll probably be doing more harm than good, so here's how to indulge your way to a spiritual awakening.

---

* We are. We are laughing at your sneakers.

THE HEALTH RISKS OF NOT TREATING YOURSELF

Are you letting yourself be bad once in a while? If not, you could be hurting your health. Little sumptuous moments you steal for yourself in an easy chair with your eyes closed aren't just for fun—as a woman, you need to indulge occasionally in order for your system to function properly. Here are some ways you may not be treating yourself and the scary health problems you could be risking as a result:

- *Not enough chocolate:* cancer from lack of pleasure
- *Only one glass of wine:* depression due to not enough wine
- *Bubbleless bath:* death from exposure to your unbubbled, naked body
- *Holding a mug of tea with just one cupped hand:* scalding burns
- *Biting into something with your eyes open:* anxiety and suicide due to loss of savoring, being in the moment, and slowing down

Drink wine!

Everybody knows that the most important way to "live a little" is with the nectar of the goddesses: wine! Wine loosens us up so we can become more empathetic and caring and also a little horny. Wine is the thing that gets us up in the morning and tucks us in at night. Wine is like a warm hug or a good friend who keeps you grounded and constantly reminds you that wine is awesome. A trendy bottle of wine with a name like "Mama's Reserve," "Sauvy B Bad," or "Bitch Juice" is the first crucial step in preparing yourself, physically and emotionally, to find spiritual enlightenment in order to help others. Also, it's a crazy world out there, so you should probably be a little drunk before you deal with it.

Take offense.

Now it's time to channel that passion for Pinot into figuring out what grinds your gears—namely, who is doing something offensive. Being offended by others lets them know how wrong they are and can leave you with a feeling of deep satisfaction. "Did you know that soda is killing millions of people every day? Even the so-called artisanal stuff," you might say. Then watch your friends drop their glass bottles of 90-calorie grapefruit soda. "You're gonna recycle that, right?" you might say, and they'll pick it up out of the trash, run to the nearest recycling center, and repent until they are clean.

Once you've started building awareness for a variety of problems, your less enlightened friends will look to you to know when they should applaud a cause or be appalled by it. This is your power. It feels amazing, but do not abuse it. Take breaks to meditate on how right you are.

Promote awareness.

So let's say you've practiced adequate self-care, have a good buzz going, and are feeling #offended enough to help others, but you don't have time to leave the country or the money for our $350-per-head gala dinner hosted by Gloria Steinem's cousin. It's okay; we can't all be rich!* You still have the power to build #awareness for a cause. Building awareness is the next best thing to doing concrete, meaningful work and is a great way to share your opinions about the problems that you don't have the time to actively solve right now. Who knows—if the right people see your outrage about Syrian refugees or which celebrity-endorsed mois- turizer is using cheap ingredients, they might be #inspired to come to our gala and help fix it with their money. It's really a shame you can't come to our gala! At least you have wine.

Now get out there and buy something!

You don't have a lot of time in your busy schedule, and shopping is never easy, but it defi- nitely just got easier. With some of the coolest brands committing themselves to ending global poverty with 1 percent of your purchase, spending your money the right way has

THIS WOMAN paid $250 just to let an endangered dolphin kiss her cheek in Cozumel, Mexico.

---

* Especially Brenna. We do *not* know why she became a social worker.

never been more effortless. Sure, it still takes some work to know which lingerie companies are hiring child sweatshop labor or taking advantage of young women in Pakistan, but fortunately many brands are happy to tell you what you want to hear with their hip, engaging marketing promises. Corporations are people too, and some people are just nicer than others. Now that's what we call "making a difference"!

Show #gratitude for the things you have.

In the end, steering the universe toward truth and justice is no easy task. But it's important to be grateful for the abilities, strength, and blessings that allow you to do so. After all, showing #gratitude actually makes you *feel* more grateful, and even inspires more #gratitude in others. Even women with very little to be grateful for can benefit from your gratitude! How nice of you!

No doubt about it, changing the world and changing yourself are going to take a *lot* of work. The question remains: "Do I go to the gym today, or do I fix human trafficking?" The choice

LITTLE THINGS YOU CAN DO TO SAVE THE WORLD

Plenty of busy feminists on the go have found creative ways to make a difference in the world—*without* dumping their fiancés and joining the Peace Corps. We call each of these efforts a "micro-good," and at the end of the day, they really add up!

Examples:

- Riding your bike to work instead of carpooling
- Sharing a meme about poverty!
- Asking for a plastic cup of tap water instead of bottled water
- Reusing plastic bags!
- Smiling at an old woman on the street
- Thinking about elephants!

All of these things can make the world a better place, without costing you any vacation days. After all, you can't save the world unless you get some rest once in a while!

is yours, but it's totally understandable if you really need to go to the gym. The important thing to know is that if you are reading this book right now, you have the power to make a difference. You got this! This section will give you lots of inspiration to transform your world, but mostly *you*.

FIND YOUR LIFESTYLE GURU

Some of the greatest activists of our time are helping women around the world to focus on self-care and to make every aspect of their lives lovely. Here are a few who can help you help yourself first.

Gwyneth Paltrow

Gwynnie shows women that it's no crime to be rich and indulgent *and* not afraid to show it; in fact, she's selflessly helping other people do it too! Her shining example helps other women know where to get the purest deer-fat candles, the most charming automatic nut-milk maker, and the healthiest vegan toast. She's giving to herself in order to give back! If you enjoy cataloging all of your joys in order for others to see what their lives could be, Gwyneth is the guru for you.

Martha Stewart

Stewart has built a career on helping women be better by letting them indulge in their most obsessive and expensive homemaking routines. Don't we all deserve that! And this woman hasn't let her humbling life experiences, including a five-month prison stay for insider trading, get in the way of her mission to help others. If you'd rather spend eleven hours making the perfect Christmas ornament for your family than spend that time with them, Stewart is the master homemaker for you.

Marie Kondo

Author of the classic *The Life-Changing Magic of Tidying Up,* Marie Kondo shows that the best way to show appreciation for your overabundant possessions is by just throwing a bunch of them out. She gives you real, philosophical justifications for color-organizing your t-shirts and what makes your stack of books unhappy. If you are seeking meaning in every object you own because you can't find it anywhere else in your life, Marie Kondo is your go-to guru.

PROBLEMATIC PRODUCTS

As you're going about your feminist journey, attempting to nourish your insides and out-sides, it's natural to want to purchase a variety of products to help you on your way. Go for it! But wait—are the products you're buying deeply problematic? Check this list to make sure the products you buy support feminism and promote social responsibility!

Harmful	Helpful
Bananas: Banana farmers aren't paid fair wages. Buying this fruit is like supporting slavery!	**Organic bananas:** They are much better for you!
Native American headdresses: This one should be obvious. It's insanely insensitive to appropriate a part of someone's culture just because you think it's cute.	**Tribal print leggings:** These are okay to buy because they are hella cute!! No one would blame you. How could you resist those delicious little zigzags?
Diet Coke: This carbonated chemical-laden death drink is full of carcinogens!	**Coke Zero!:** Scientists haven't had enough time to study what Coke Zero does to a raw steak just yet, so for now, it's a solid purchase!
Chemical laxatives: Buying and using laxatives to lose weight is a gateway to an eating disorder. This is unhealthy and we're worried about you.	*Garcinia cambogia:* This miracle fruit is Dr. Oz–approved, which means it's totally okay to use as a laxative! Dr. Oz is, after all, a Dr.!
iPhones: They are made in horrible factories!	**Samsung Galaxy phones:** They are made in, like, amazing factories!
BIC "For Her" pens: Um, what? Since when do women need a pink version of a product used by both sexes, just for the sake of jacking up the cost?	**BIC "For Women" Soleil razors:** This razor is strong enough for a woman!

Harmful	Helpful
Bottled water: Not only are these products rarely sourced responsibly, they also create a major, unnecessary strain on the waste stream!	**Feelings Water:** It's bottled water, but for charity, y'all! See our advertorial on page 196 for more info!
Tom's of Maine toothpaste: It's immoral to present your company as a folksy-dolksy mom-and-pop shop when you're actually affiliated with a major corporation.	**TOMS shoes:** They're so down-to-earth and normcore!
The Help: Typical whitewashing! This book makes it seem like whites *helped* black people in the Jim Crow South instead of being the reason they were oppressed.	*The Help* on **DVD:** Emma Stone is so great tho!! And it was on sale!!
Quinoa: This grain, once a staple of Bolivian cuisine, is now so expensive due to Western demand that the people who harvest it can no longer afford it. Even quinoa marked as "fair-trade" doesn't change the fact that natives do not have access to this complete protein that's indigenous to their land.	**Fair-trade quinoa:** But it's gotta be like a *little* bit better, right?
Peanut butter: Dangerous for people with allergies!	**Almond butter:** Delicious!
Chris Brown tickets: Chris Brown is violent toward women!!!	**Tickets to an NFL game:** Just some good old-fashioned fun here!

Womanera Shoes

Buy a Pair, Buy Another Pair, Give a Pair

With every pair of heels you purchase, Womanera will donate one heel to a child in need. So go ahead—buy another pair!

Womanera is a shoe company here to change the world. We know that children need shoes to walk to school and to build confidence. And nothing builds confidence more than heels. That's why we've made world-changing, comfortable high-heeled shoes that can take you from day to night— *and* take a child out of poverty—*in heels.*

Why not flats? Because you are a woman and you like the way heels make your butt look. Why would a child deserve any less than you do?

Also, we make heels. We don't make flats. Flats are gross.

Heels are actually pretty expensive. Which is why we can only afford to donate one heel for every pair you buy. So you should probably buy another pair. You don't want a child walking around with just one heel, do you?

But it doesn't stop there. Once all the children in the world have all the shoes they could ever want, we'll devote 100 percent of our time to finding another trending charity cause.

Check out our sister brand, Bagera,

WHERE EVERY BAG PURCHASE GOES TOWARD GIVING SINGLE MOMS JOBS MAKING BAGS.

TRADING IN ORIGINAL SIN FOR KARMA!

Our prudish, puritanical culture can keep you from harnessing your true feminine energy. Western practices have taught us that we women are born broken and in need of saving, and our miserable existence is punishment for our sinful nature. Luckily, more holistic Eastern philosophies, like Hinduism and Buddhism, include the idea of karmic retribution, which shows that we're simply suffering for our own mistakes—mistakes made of our own beautiful free will! Here's how to ditch the dogma of the Bible and get spiritual with Eastern traditions that nurture rather than punish.* Cast off the shackles of outdated religions and relish the beauty of *ancient* religions!

Don't blame Eve. Blame yourself.

The Christian idea that our sole female ancestor, Eve, was to blame for the fall of man, our collective guilt, and the need for human suffering on earth sounds pretty anti-women, if you ask us! Luckily, the idea of karma allows us to take responsibility for our suffering and see it as the result of bad deeds we may have performed in this life or in past lives. When we each collectively shoulder that burden as spiritual beings, women look a lot better and more responsible on the whole. Now we can finally learn to embrace the pain of childbirth!

Don't go to church. Go to yoga.

Unlike sitting in a church pew, yoga positions allow you to stretch your muscles and your mind in the process. It's great to have a spiritual practice that's freeing instead of restrictive! So rather than rigidly confessing your sins, learn the flowing yoga postures.

Can't get into that posture? Your stiff upper back is probably due to a blocked heart chakra, meaning you haven't been loving enough toward your fellow creatures. Luckily you can release that tension *and* your karma through more yoga! Just make sure you go at least twice a week for full benefits and do the poses in the correct sequence and don't eat beforehand and make sure you drink plenty of water and keep your body free from impurities and have compassion for all living things and try to ditch the blocks as soon as you can.

---

* Or only punish when appropriate.

Now you're celebrating and respecting your feminine energy by focusing on feeling better here and now* rather than striving to achieve some form of perfection in the future!

Instead of being virginal, be celibate.

Western churches worship the purity of the virgin Mary and consequentially shame women for promiscuity and "fleshly desires." Talk about patriarchal! Thankfully, the more forgiving philosophy of Buddhism has a different take on sexuality. According to its Five Precepts, one should do one's best to avoid sensuality and lust. This idea places the responsibility in your hands to remain pure in order to attain *jhana,* or higher awareness, rather than being shamed by an angry God for falling short of his majesty. Transcendent!

Don't pray. Chant!

Instead of reciting Hail Marys over and over like some uptight, moralistic nun, get in touch with your spiritual side through Buddhist chanting. Repeating the mantra *Nam Myoho Renge Kyo* is a daily practice that, unlike rote prayers, allows the chanter to attain perfect and complete awakening. So instead of asking the "blessed" Mary to "pray for us sinners," you're now "taking refuge in the Wonderful Law of the Lotus Flower Sutra." It just makes more sense in a modern feminist context!

You're never gonna find *nirvana* in traditional (strict) Christian customs, but you will in the devoted practices of Buddhism and Hinduism (doesn't matter which!). So ditch those stuffy old beliefs for these even older religions and get with the times!

CHARITY MAD LIBS

Not sure what charity you should be running? Just use your life experience to figure out which cause is most meaningful to you! Maybe your life story is "I've always liked dolphins so now I help dolphins," or, "I heard a fact about carbon emissions that made me nervous," or even "One time I saw a poor person, and it made me sad." Don't have a backstory ready? Use this handy "mad lib" to help you figure it out!

---

* While also living the consequences of any mistakes you've made in this life or others.

CHARITY MAD LIBS

I grew up in a/an _____ town, the daughter of a/an _____ and a/an

ADJECTIVE ... PROFESSION

_____. My _____ sisters and I had an idyllic childhood: _____,

TYPE OF WOMAN ... NUMBER ... SPORT

_____, _____ every summer at the _____ house,

OTHER SPORT ... OUTDOOR MEAL, PLURAL ... TYPE OF BODY OF WATER

even a little healthy experimentation with _____. It was an all-American up-

SOMETHING FUN

bringing. When I entered college at _____ to study _____, I had

UNIVERSITY ... SOME BULLSHIT DEGREE

never even thought about _____. I figured people who dealt with that were just

TYPE OF HARDSHIP

_____, or at least _____. Either way, I didn't think it was my

NEGATIVE ADJECTIVE ... LESS NEGATIVE ADJECTIVE

problem. Then, everything changed: I studied abroad in _____.

FOREIGN COUNTRY

As soon as I stepped off the _____, _____ was everywhere.

TYPE OF TRANSPORTATION ... TYPE OF HARDSHIP

Entire families went without _____ for weeks. One little boy was so

SOMETHING YOU USE EVERY DAY

_____, he had to share his _____ with his _____

ADJECTIVE ... SOMETHING A CHILD WOULD HAVE ... NUMBER ABOVE 8

siblings. Everyone I met was affected by this _____, but they would tell

SYNONYM FOR "SCOURGE"

me it was just part of life in their village, the village of _____town. I knew I had

BORING GUY NAME

to do something.

It started with just one _____. I built it with my friends

TYPE OF BUILDING, TECHNOLOGY, OR PRODUCT

_____ and _____ with the help of the villagers. They were hesitant at

THE NAME "BRITA" ... THE NAME "GEORGE"

first, but once they used it, they knew I was a/an _____ person and thanked me

ADJECTIVE

accordingly. Seeing all of them _____ and _____, I felt

VERB ENDING IN -ING ... ANOTHER VERB ENDING IN -ING

like I had just scored a goal in _____. I knew right then that helping others

FIRST SPORT, FROM BEFORE

wasn't just a/an _____ hobby; it was the purpose of my life.

ADJECTIVE

That was _____ years ago, and since then we have grown by leaps and

NUMBER UNDER 7

_____. Now, _____ the _____, as we call it, has built over

NOUN, PLURAL ... VERB ENDING IN -ING ... NOUN

50,000 _____ worldwide, helping millions of

TYPE OF BUILDING, TECHNOLOGY, OR PRODUCT FROM BEFORE, PLURAL

children to achieve their dream of _____ and, in turn, helping me achieve

THING PEOPLE DREAM ABOUT

my dream of helping other people achieve their dreams.

Thank you, _____. But more important, thank *me*.

NAME OF FOREIGN COUNTRY FROM BEFORE

Pink Goats International

Most charities help people, but few charities really own helping people. That's why we at Pink Goats International—an incredible organization that seeks to end hunger, alleviate rural poverty, and spread the sassy—give thousands of pink goats every year to women in not-American countries who are making a difference in their communities.

Farm animals like goats provide milk, meat, fiber, and labor, making them a reliable source of income for anyone anywhere. And the color pink provides a feeling of *Oooooh baby hell yeah! Zap zap zap booooom! Gimme more baby yaaasss!!! Mmmmm ha ha ha women are cool.*

"That's why PGI gives them pink goats," says Morris Gutmore, the CEO of Gutmore Chemicals, the company responsible for the massive spill near a goat farm back in 2014. "That's the reason for the pink goats."

Here's how it works. For every $75 donation, PGI will give one pink goat to a kickass woman who's doing great stuff in a country that seems warm.

Meet Bernadette.

She bought a goat with a microloan from a bank started by women in her community. "This goat provides me with milk that I make into cheese and soap that I sell at the market," says Bernadette. "I can afford to send my children to a private school and get medical treatment for my mother."

You may see this and think, "Wow, maybe large-scale international charities *aren't* the answer. Maybe these people just need to not be colonized for hundreds of years to have a shot at a better life."

But we thought, "Wait—what if that goat were pink?"

Wow.

I mean.

That goat!

It's pink!

"I don't understand," says Bernadette, clearly overwhelmed with gratitude. "What have you done with my goat? This goat is male. I cannot milk him. Why is he pink?"

Wow.

Bernadette now has a pink goat, whereas before she did not. And *that's* the difference.

It's our distinct honor and privilege to have provided so many women with so many pink goats.

For more info on our amazing her-spiring pink program, go to www.pinkgoats.org.

INSPIRING MEMES TO SHARE WITH YOUR FRIENDS!

It can be hard for women to stay inspired day to day. So what do you do when you've already powered up with a green smoothie and still need a little *oomph* to get you through the day? Look at inspiring Internet memes, that's what! You've seen them all over Facebook, Pinterest, and Instagram, but sometimes there just aren't enough out there to get you where you need to be inspiration-wise. Here's how to create your own, in a pinch, to share with friends via social media.

Find an image.

Your image should be just as uplifting as the message placed upon it. Think photos of nature, food, or a woman with her hands stretched out. *Examples:*

Find a quote.

Quotes can be defined as any sentence that has been posted online. Do a quick Google search for anything, and copy and paste any sentence into your quote doc. It doesn't have to be by a famous person either. The first rule of inspirational quotes is that it doesn't matter who said them as long as they have a positive message. *Examples:*

"You are a sparkling sparkle, and no one can put you out."

"I'm a dreamer, and I'll get laid or die trying."

"Be yourself, or else you have a personality disorder, lol."

"Thank you for your purchase."

"Laugh like no one hates your weird laugh."

"Thoughts lead to words, which lead to actions. Think real good."

"I never knew what kindness was until I won a raffle."

"Don't just sit there. Start hitchhiking to your success sun."

Pair the quote with a famous person.

Select the name of someone who's rich, wise, famous, or hot and then pair that name with your chosen quote. *Examples:*

Madonna

Mother Teresa

Picasso

Rumi

Kahlil Gibran

Maya Angelou

Mark Cuban

Remember, when it comes to inspiring memes, nobody's checking facts, so don't be afraid to say what you feel using someone else's words! We're talking about gaining motivation at all costs, so don't worry about whether any of these people said any of these things. Eyes on the prize, girl!

Bring it all together!

Now slap that quote onto the image. There are a number of apps and sites that will help you do this, but we recommend Reductress's OMG That's So True, which you can find in the app store. *Examples:*

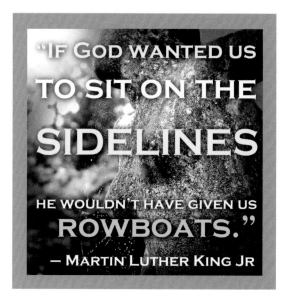

Phew! Now that you've created your own inspiring memes, you can rest assured that you're not just becoming a better feminist; you're becoming a better *person*, which is the next best thing. Good luck!

ESSENTIAL OIL BLENDS TO BRING OUT YOUR FEMININE ESSENCE

A unique feminine essence is inside every one of us; all we have to do is find it. You can spend years in search of this secret she-power, or you can coax it to the surface with the magic of essential oils. Essential oils can inspire a positive emotional state and bring out the nurturing, creative, fertile souls inside us all. Terratincta™ offers a line of feminurturing essential-oil blends that will help you survive and thrive for another day of saving the world.

White Savoiria™

White Savoiria is a blend of vanilla and lavender oils perfect for daily use for the type of woman who calls out the politically incorrect transgressions of bots on Twitter. This blend can be rubbed on skin and hair in order to nourish your roots, nurture your complexion, and calm your spirit after a long day of social-justice warrioring online.

Voluntourisma™

Eucalyptus, frankincense, and jasmine oils combine to form this aromatic blend that will help empower you to visit third-world countries to paint murals and take photos of yourself with poor children. Rub it on your feet after a long day of hiking up Machu Picchu to strengthen and calm your nerves for another day of taking in others' experiences as a privileged outsider. Remember, if you weren't there doing the work for free, there'd be locals doing that job for a living wage. You are helping!

Protestia™

Peppermint, lemon, and orange oils awaken your senses in this oil blend that will get you going for an early morning of shouting at passersby on the street. Whether you're upset about the location of the new mall or the lack of candle offerings at the new mall, this blend can be inhaled deeply to activate regions in the limbic system associated with emotion, helping you to get in touch with why you're so upset by the state of the world.

Essential oils have been used since ancient times by busy women who were finally making time to treat themselves for once. Get in touch with the pure essences of the earth while getting in touch with yourself, who is a good, good person.

SMOKING POT IS FEMINIST TOO, MAN

Dude, you might not think so, but smoking pot is definitely feminist. Saving the world is about being green, and what's more green than marijuana (lol)? Seriously though, smoking reefer helps people in a number of ways.

Glaucoma or Some Shit

If you have eye problems, you're gonna want some pot. Do you want to deny people with sick eyes the stuff that helps them? No, you're a loving, feminist, chill soul. If you want to help people, you should be pro-weed.

Other Parts of Your Body That Hurt

Does something on your body hurt? That fucking *suuuuuucks*. Lots of other people have parts of their bodies that hurt, and smoking weed can make them hurt less and also make them super into *Bob's Burgers* even if they don't normally like it. Helping people is feminist, and you can help people by smoking weed with them.

Anxiety/Depression/Bummers

Nothing gets a mentally stuck person back in the flow like a good toke. If you're into a happy world and happy people and just like equality and all that, you should def support the green stuff.

   (Finish the rest of this later, remember to buy cereal.)

THINGS YOU CAN PROTEST BY TAKING YOUR TOP OFF

There are so many things to protest out there, and just as many that you can protest by taking your top off. Taking your top off is a great way to bring attention to a cause and also to yourself. Why not have a little fun while drawing a crowd for the *right* reasons? Here are some things you can protest by shaking those mamms!

Fracking

Animal testing

Tax breaks for the rich

Tuition hikes

Monsanto

Guns

New condos being built anywhere

Cable-company monopoly

Gratuitous nudity on HBO

Rent increases on your local cupcake business

The new footpath around the lake

Loud cars

Low literacy rates

Football concussion risks

Shirts

Bras

A CELEBRATION OF BUTT-WALK

Why are all these women backing it up? Butt-Walk is a 10K in which women celebrate their big beautiful behinds and fight against butt-shaming by walking or running the whole route backward, or "Ass first or be cursed," as the chant goes. Sign up for your local Butt-Walk at butt-walk.org.

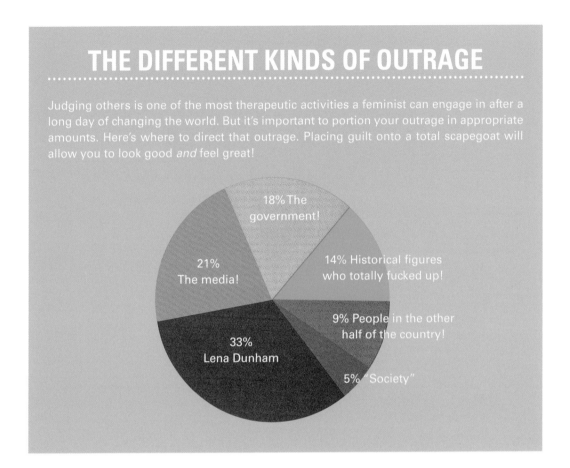

THE DIFFERENT KINDS OF OUTRAGE

Judging others is one of the most therapeutic activities a feminist can engage in after a long day of changing the world. But it's important to portion your outrage in appropriate amounts. Here's where to direct that outrage. Placing guilt onto a total scapegoat will allow you to look good *and* feel great!

18% The government!

14% Historical figures who totally fucked up!

21% The media!

9% People in the other half of the country!

33% Lena Dunham

5% "Society"

PRACTICING SELF-LOVE ON OTHER PEOPLE

In our broken, patriarchal society, we women are taught to be highly critical of our bodies, our abilities—and even our thoughts!* As a woman, you may not be naturally inclined to put your own happiness first and really *love* yourself. Maybe you never even *pictured* loving yourself. You might just not be that into yourself! I mean, you're you! You could do better, right? You're barely even *friends* with yourself. However, with a little practice, you can eventually learn to settle for yourself: the sweet, funny, supportive girl who's been there for you all along.

Here's how to learn self-love by testing out your self-love skills on other people.

---

* We're our own thought police! Dystopia is *now,* bitches!

Give love to someone you hate—besides yourself.

You're not going to grow if you're not challenging yourself, and trust us, loving yourself will be a *challenge*. So pick someone who's hard to love and who generally doesn't appreciate you, like a perennial ex-boyfriend who treats you badly but lives nearby and never says no. Do little things for him that make him feel loved, like leaving love notes near his at-home tattoo equipment, or making him a gluten-free vegan lunch bowl, or feeding his rat. Now, picture yourself doing all these things for yourself. They may not be things you would enjoy or even like, but hey—baby steps!

Tell everyone you meet, "It's not your fault."

Forgiveness is like little bottles of hotel shampoo—you'll never run out! The most important thing most of us overworked ladies need to realize is that inner peace is not a finite resource. The more you give, the more you have!

As an exercise, pick a day and for everyone you encounter, take them by the shoulders, stare meaningfully into their eyes, and give them the forgiveness you wish you could give yourself. To your barista, say, "Mom and Dad's divorce was not your fault." To the bus driver: "You couldn't have stopped that fire by being a better person. That's not how fire works." To your intern at work: "You did *not* turn Ken gay. Ken was *always* gay." Once you see how pouring out your love actually makes your love jug bigger, maybe you'll be able to give a little teeny tiny cup of love to yourself.

If you're feeling depressed, ask a friend if they need help.

When you're struggling with anxiety or low self-esteem, it can easily spiral into full-on depression. It may feel as though everyone around you is doing fine and accomplishing amazing things, while you're barely functioning on a basic level. Even small tasks like brushing your hair can feel insurmountable. Everything is consumed by your own self-hatred and despair, and you wonder if you'd be better off dead.

At times like this, it's important to reach out to your friends to see how you can help them. Be there for them however you can, being careful not to let any of your dumb problems stress them out. Maybe they're moving in with their fiancé and need someone to watch the U-Haul. Maybe they're a little unsure of the wording of an e-mail to their new PR person. Maybe they can't quite open a jar of capers. Whatever it is, practice being there for them, so that you can someday be there for yourself. Eventually, you'll be able to open your *own* capers.

Write a letter to an attractive celebrity.

Numerous studies have shown that attractive people are believed to be more worthy of love and, in fact, *are* more worthy of love. Close your eyes and picture your face. Now, make your eyes bigger. Make your chin smaller. Erase your nose. Add little lens flares next to your cheeks. Now replace that image with Emma Stone's face. Pretend you are Emma Stone. Take a walk in her face. Wow. Nice having a nice face, right?

Send her a thank-you card, care of her agency in Beverly Hills, telling her all the things you wish you could tell yourself, like, "Your lip scar makes you beautiful," or "People say they can't even *see* your lip scar," or "Your lip scar is not your fault." This will not affect what your actual face looks like, but if you do it every day, it should help, right?

Masturbate for someone.

Self-love isn't just a euphemism for being healthy; it's also a euphemism for diddling yourself. But before you can love yourself, you have to love yourself to someone else. Touch someone's genitals for them until they say, "Unnghhh." Doesn't that feel good? Once you feel comfortable doing this for someone else, try it on yourself. The best way to feel deserving of sexual satisfaction by yourself is by letting someone else feel that satisfaction!

Once you're mastered all these exercises, you are finally ready to start loving yourself. Now get to it before someone does it better than you!

THE TOP TEN WAYS TO KNOW IF YOU REALLY LOVE YOURSELF

Not sure if your self-love has taken hold just yet? Ask yourself these questions to know for sure:

1. Is your mantra just your own name? _____

2. If someone asked you, "Who is your biggest hero?" would you even hesitate to say, "Me"? _____

3. When was the last time you hugged yourself? _____

4. How about the last time you kissed yourself? _____

5. You *do* know how to kiss yourself, right? _____

6. Have you ever lip-synched along to "The Wind Beneath My Wings" while gazing into a mirror? _____

7. When you sneeze in a room by yourself, do you say, "Bless me"? _____

8. How many times a day do you stop right where you are, look at the world around you, smile softly, and think, "You're welcome, everyone"? _____

9. When you bite into a square of chocolate, do you imagine the chocolate saying, "Mmm"? _____

10. Have you ever reached orgasm, by accident, just from catching a glimpse of yourself in a store window? _____

Meditate on the answers above and see if they reflect feelings of pure unadulterated self-love. Do you know you're worth it?

OVERCOME YOUR WOMINSECURITIES WITH CRYSTALS!

Normal adults can solve their problems with a little critical thinking and know-how. But you're a woman. You don't need skills to solve your problems—you can use crystals! The magical properties of these amazing nature rocks can help us girls with any struggle we're having, no matter how tough. And we *don't* just mean generally, like anxiety or depression or finding inner truth. We mean *very specifically* and *for real*!! Here are some little-known uses for the world's most powerful crystals:

AMBER: Amber is not just the name of the girl you used to shoplift with; it's also the name of a healing crystal! Its yellow vibes can soothe a variety of life-interrupting ailments, including hangovers, fibromyalgia, polycystic ovary syndrome, and not really "getting" Sigur Rós.

AMETHYST: The cleansing purples of amethyst are a natural aid for anyone stuck in a loveless marriage. Put an amethyst under his pillow to make him love you again!

CITRINE: Citrine helps usher in abundance and energy, both useful for spending enough money to get over guys named Seth. Put one in your wallet!

CLEAR QUARTZ: Quartz is a versatile crystal that can be programmed for just about anything—like cleansing your body of toxins before a surprise drug test!

HEMATITE: Hematite can help fix your low credit rating.

JADE: Jade is revered for allowing access to spiritual, creative forces and gaining insight. Let it help you figure out why your period hurts like shit!

JASPER: Known as the "nurturing stone," jasper can help you stop hating your thighs.

LAPIS LAZULI: Lapis can help open the throat chakra, allowing you to speak your truth when you're afraid to speak up at work because your boss just purchased a large decorative sword.

MALACHITE: A powerful protection stone, malachite can be used for when you're afraid that everything Steve said to you in that e-mail was right, even though he can't hold down a job and is high most of the time.

MOONSTONE: Moonstone helps you get in touch with feminine sensuality when you're having difficulty orgasming outside of a bathtub.

ONYX: Onyx imparts self-confidence and strength for when you just got hit by a car and everyone saw—even your crush!!!

ROSE QUARTZ: Rose quartz helps the wearer get in touch with unconditional love at stressful times, like when you hate how bad you are at putting on liquid eyeliner.

TIGER'S EYE: Tiger's eye stabilizes mood swings; it's good for when you just realized you have cellulite on your arms.

Don't let fundamental wominsecurities get in the way of finding your true feminine power—with crystals!

Feature: LYLA STEINGARD-HOPE ON HER SERIES OF AHA! MOMENTS

Aha! Moment: *n.* A sudden realization, the moment when everything becomes clear.

We spoke with Lyla Steingard-Hope, former CEO and current life coach, who shared with us the story of her series of Aha! Moments.

My first Aha! Moment was actually more of a series of tiny Aha!s that came together to create the singular Aha! Moment that I call *my life*.

I used to be glued to my Eames chair, working like a madwoman seven days a week. I was making more money than you could possibly imagine (go ahead, I dare you) and living an otherwise "happy" and "fulfilled" life. But one day I asked myself, "Lyla, are you living the life you had imagined?" As I felt the ample sunlight in my corner office, I thought, "The life I imagine is only as real as the life I'm truly living."

Aha! That was the moment that changed everything. It was the moment everything *made sense.* Then I threw the keys to my corner office out the twenty-second-floor window, said good-bye to nobody in particular, and packed my backpack for the Andes.

It was exactly as simple as it sounds.

So what is it that makes an Aha! Moment? Well, let's break it down to its essential parts.

"_____"

This is the part that comes right before your Aha! Moment. Always take a moment to breathe. *For in the stillness, you find truth.*

A

This is the first and most important part of the Aha! Moment. It is the backswing of your "ha!" This is where you wait comfortably and patiently for the Aha!, because *manifesting requires detachment.*

Ha!

This is it: the crowning syllable of your Aha! Moment. This is you saying "Ha!" in the face of not realizing your potential as a woman. *Sit in gratitude of all that is crystallizing around you,* for without the exclamation point this "Ha!" is nothing but a "Ha."

See how that felt? Amazing, right?

Moment

Aha! This is the actual moment you are experiencing right now. Without this moment, there would be no time or space for your "Aha!" to fill. It will leave you as quickly as a thief in the night, so you must savor the flash of realization as it comes to you. Separate out the syllables: "mo-ment." Can you feel it? Can you feel the Aha! resonating in this moment? *The time that is now is the time we have here.*

"_____"

This is the following moment, where you pause to let the weight of the previous moment settle in.

So what exactly led me to my Aha! Moment? Well, let me tell you: *the things that lead us where we need to be were there all along.* Aha! I'm sorry; I just had another Aha! Moment. They come so often now, like spiritual sneezes.

Anyway, there I was, backpacking through the Andes after quitting a $700,000-a-year job. As I summited my third peak of the day, I thought, "I could really go for a rich, chocolatey frozen dessert right now. But there's not a froyo place in sight." And then I remembered: *the only things that are in front of us are the things we believe are there.*

And that's when everything changed—again. Three weeks later, I manifested the first froyo shop in the Andes. Who would have thought the mountain folk would love froyo so much? *I did. For we are all one, and your feelings are also mine.*

My budding relationship with the mountain folk led me to become aware of many issues in the area—deforestation, oil companies taking control of the politics in the region, ancient tribes losing their heritage—it sounded like a recipe for disaster, one that the developed world was actively choosing to ignore.

"Can you call your good friend Bill Gates and get him to help? Our fish population has plummeted, and we have nothing to eat," one of their leaders asked me.

"I could give a man a fish," I said. "Or I could teach a man to have an Aha! Moment."

They nodded and smiled, and in their own native tongue they exclaimed, "Aha! I should tweet that! That was a good one."

After teaching the local mountain folk first what an Aha! Moment was and then how to turn their own Aha! Moments into *meaningful change in their lives,* they thanked me for showing them the path to self-realization. *I did it. Me.* Aha!

And that's when I realized: my entire life is just a series of Aha! Moments piled on top of each other. I am a wellspring of self-realization. *I need to write a book.* Aha!

Now that my book, *Putting the Aha! Back in the Moment,* has sold its first million copies, I've quietly realized that so many people are capable of taking charge of their own lives, one Aha! Moment after another Aha! Moment at a time. You can do it, *if you just Aha! hard enough.*

Feelings Water

In many rural parts of India, tens of millions of people contract life-threatening water-borne illnesses every year. That's what makes Pratima R. and her invention all the more incredible.

"I have always loved science and am always tinkering," she says. "I thought maybe I could be an engineer someday."

That someday is now. At just fifteen years old, Pratima created the most efficient low-cost biodegradable water filter ever invented. It removes up to 99.99 percent of pollutants like bacteria and even heavy metals.

"I know many people who have become sick with diarrhea and missed school or work, and even one boy in my class who died," she explains softly. "I am happy my idea can help many people."

Engineers in New Delhi are working to distribute the plans to create the filter, which is easily constructed with cotton, charcoal, and a few simple household objects. "Pratima is the kind of genius who comes around once or twice in a generation," says Aneeth Kannan, an engineer on the project.

And that's exactly why the makers of Feelings™ Water sent Pratima to modeling school in Paris! For six months, she'll live with twenty other talented teenagers from around the globe and learn how to walk, pose, and *werk* from the best modeling coaches in the world. This way, she can learn to *love herself* and *feel confident in her own skin*. Because that's what being a remarkable woman is all about.

"I don't understand," says Pratima. "Why did you send me here? There's no schooling, and I'm not tall enough."

We can't wait to see Pratima develop some confidence!

LIFE-CHANGING BOOKS THAT WILL *CHANGE YOUR LIFE*

Need something to jump-start your life? There's a book for that! Not just any book though. After you finish this book, here are some other books that will *change your fucking life.* Up your enlightened feminist game with these inspiring, existence-affirming reads that we treasure and worship every day of our blessed lives.

Wake Up: Awakening to the Wakefulness That Is Your Waking Life

We don't think there's anything more important than awakening. From the genius mind of Rory Chenk, spiritual guru and host of the show *Wake Up!,* this self-help tome will help you "wake up" to the awakening happening around you, so you can take the first wakeful step on the long journey that is your waking life. We fucking love this book!

Oops, We Fell Off a Cliff

Based on the unbelievable story of Will and Gina Quinlan, this is the harrowing account of how this brave couple fell in love, climbed a cliff, and accidentally fell off that cliff into a ravine, where they were forced to use their own inner strength to survive six harrowing years trapped in an even deeper ravine. Will and Gina share some of the valuable lessons they learned during those chilling years. This inspiring story will leave you breathless, just as it did Will and Gina, who somehow lived to tell the story.*

How to Find Your Inner Child and Put Her to Work

You've spent years of your adult life finding your inner child. Now what? Khalil Na-Tamasa's self-help tome will help you find ways to make your inner child highly effective at work and at home. Your inner child reminded you to have a sense of play, but now it's time to train her to become a responsible, productive member of society, just like you.

Loud

At twenty-seven, Marnie Heifer was lost. After three shattered marriages, a layoff, and getting into a weird fight with her mailman, she decides to leave her old life behind to embark upon

---

* Unfortunately, we recently found out that Will and Gina did not actually fall off a cliff and that the story was entirely fabricated. They apologize for the misunderstanding, but that does *not* make this book any less life-changing!

a journey across the wilds of America, screaming, yelling, shrieking, blasting loud music, and doing it all by herself. Marnie experiences catharsis through the emotional and raw cross-country screaming adventure, learning a lot about herself along the way. This is the story of a young woman letting go of her past and finding her voice in the quest for inner peace. Spoiler alert: we are living in an entirely different parallel universe after reading this book!

Stillness in Dance

In this revolutionary look at the world of dance, Lily Mannette details why her favorite moments are the ones in which the dancers aren't moving at all and why we in the dance of life need not even attempt to dance. After reading this book, you'll never want to dance again! We sure don't!

The Time I Fucked a Tan Guy

After an alcohol-fueled trip to Myrtle Beach, Tami Wysocki wrote a memoir detailing the most pivotal moment in her life: fucking a guy who was really tan. Like, *really* tan. This is the first-person account of how Tami broke all the rules and fucked a really tan guy just one time and was *forever changed*. We keep this book underneath our pillow in the hopes that the Book Fairy will come and give us more books like this one!

WERE YOU FEMINIST IN A PAST LIFE?

Do you ever wonder how many times you've reincarnated in a woman's body? Or what your past lives were like, and if their politics aligned with yours? It's very possible that this is not the first lifetime in which you bore the torch of feminism. Here are some tools you can use to determine whether you may have been feminist in a past life (whether or not feminism was a "thing" at that time).

Look to your dreams.

Do you have recurring dreams of marching down the streets with a group of suffragettes, singing your battle cry for access to the vote? No? How about a dream in which you light all of your bras on fire in a public act of defiance? Not really? Well, if you've ever had a dream where your teeth fell out, that could actually be a memory from a past life in which you were a beggar woman, unable to inherit property due to her lack of a husband. Since the feminist bar was set a lot lower back then, your dream may be proof that you were a totally badass feminist wench, a past-life nod to your current feminist inclinations. Cool!

Let your feelings lead you.

Have you ever visited a place and felt like you just belonged there? Was that place a central location in feminist movements of the past? Does fire scare you? It may be that you were burned at the stake in medieval times for being a woman who sought to practice medicine and was thus labeled a witch. Sounds like a pretty feminist life to us! Hot!

Do a past-life regression.

Sometimes it helps to have a professional regress you through hypnosis to a state in which you can recall your past lives. If you see yourself driving across the border in the 1960s to get a back-alley Mexican abortion, congrats—you're a reincarnated feminist. But don't worry if you end up remembering many lifetimes as a womanizing playboy. It just means you're here to make up for that karma in this life. So get to work, feminist!

Knowing you were feminist in a past life can be totally inspiring. But remember—there are still a lot of feminist things to be done in this lifetime. It's your job to shape what a feminist wench of the twenty-first century will look like!

FIND YOUR SPIRIT FEMINIST!

When forging your feminist path through the forest of patriarchy, it's important to know who your real spirit guides are. Each of us has one or more feminist totems helping us scamper along our way. Do you know who yours is? Meditate on the possibilities by connecting with the natural world of feminism and see if any of the following feminists resonate for you.

If you're not afraid to get away from the pack . . . Virginia Woolf

Do you like holing up in a room of your own? The Virginia Woolf loves to burrow and hibernate. If this sounds like you, Virginia Woolf may be your spirit feminist. Call on her for strength and guidance when you need a break from the stresses of the misogynistic world around you or you just need to howl at the moon for a while. People might be afraid of you, but don't let that keep you a-lone!

If you're good at planning during difficult times . . . Betty Friedan

Do you have a hard time keeping still and enjoy unearthing nuts of truth buried in the ground? The Betty Friedan is very active during certain times, collecting and hoarding the stories of other women for a time when their significance can be explained. She often symbolizes change, metamorphosis, and dark inner desires. If this is your feminist totem, you'll want to balance a life of scurrying around and hiding snacks with time for reflection, meditation, and eating those snacks.

If you can buck any man who tries to control you . . . Simone de Beauvoir

Do you feel like a second-class citizen, like a beast of burden, neighing for her own agency to be recognized? The Simone de Beauvoir totem reflects a sense of feeling bridled but also of holding tremendous power. If she comes to you in your dreams galloping through a field, it may mean it's time for you to break away from some of your restraints in life and take off your blinders, because deep down you are a wild animal that's meant to live free.

If you're known for your ability to transform . . . Sojourner Truth

Do you embrace the colorful possibilities of your future in spite of powerful opponents trying to snatch you up in their talons? Are you capable of a complete metamorphosis, shedding past trials and tribulations, and using your newfound freedom to lift up others?? The Sojourner Truth may seem soft and sensitive at first, but is not afraid to emerge from her chrysalis and fly toward change. This totem can be a powerful tool if you are trying to flutter into a more empowered position in life.

If you are defensive of your territory . . . Susan B. Anthony

Do you fight fiercely for your rights when cornered, clawing and scratching at your opponents? As a spirit feminist, the Susan B. Anthony represents fierce independence, often expressed in the form of throwing shade at unwelcome visitors and taking naps whenever she wants. If this feels true for you, you can call on the Susan B. Anthony to help you pounce on your desires, regardless of outside opinion.

A NOTE ON WOMEN'S INTUITION

Do you ever just feel like something's just . . . right? Or you instinctively know something without actually knowing it? Well, you *are* right—that's your women's intuition kicking in. As women, we are able to harness the power of intuitive knowing in ways that men cannot. The cycles of the moon and our menses allow us to *feel* when things are coming to us. And contrary to what the patriarchy may have told you about feelings being bad, they're not—they're good! *They help us see things that no one else can see.* This is your one true gift among many horrible curses. Just trust it.

So when you feel like you might be pregnant even though you haven't had sex in months, just go with it—embrace that panic attack! Or when you feel like your career isn't working out for you, trust when your body tells you to drop everything and get your yoga teacher's certificate. And when the entrée the waiter brings out feels wrong, even though it's exactly what you ordered, send it back! Or when you get a weird feeling that your baby is in trouble, don't hesitate to go and check on her, even if she doesn't exist. Happiness is finding what feels right for you and trusting that feeling.

Here are a few women who trusted their intuition:

"I had a feeling my husband was cheating on me, so I snooped in his e-mail. I didn't find anything, but I did find a coupon for Best Buy. Now I have new headphones."—*Petra N.*

"My doctors told me I was fine, but I couldn't get rid of this feeling that I had cancer. So I paid for an MRI out of pocket. Now I *know* I don't have cancer."—*Melanie R.*

"For years, I had this little voice in the back of my mind saying, 'Truck. Truck. Truck.' Then one day I got hit by a van."—*Amanda H.*

Wow. See what your intuition can do for you?

Plinky: The Spell Is Cast!

Well look at you now! Oh my! At last!
You're differenter, now that the spell has been cast.
You're confident, peaceful, dividing your time,
You love yourself, touch yourself, you're a perfect
    dime.
You date right, you shop right, your life is sublime,
Which brings me henceforth to the point of my
    rhyme:

You're feminist now! Hurroo! Hurray!
Today is Day 1 and the number-one day
So get out there, F-babe, and get on your way,
Farewell now, my pet! Now Plink must away!

I am an actual Feminazi. A real one.

 DISCLAIMER

We are so, so sorry.

EPILOGUE

HERE'S WHAT YOU'VE LEARNED

Wow—you made it all the way through our book! It's been a lot of fun taking this feminist journey with you, our sexy lil' reader gal.* Remember all of the good times we had? Like when we wrote that *amazing* book you just read? Oh man, we really killed it. Let's take a brief look back at everything *you* learned from *us,* but mostly what *we* taught *you.*

Feminism is bae.

Give feminism all your love, and it will love you back.

All women have lumps.

Some of them are cause for concern, but most can be worked away with a gentle exercise regimen.**

Men can also be bae.

You can love men even more now that you love yourself fully as a woman.

You can have it all.

And that includes feminism. We hope we made that clear!

You need to feel good before you can be good.

If you can't splurge on yourself, you can't splurge on the world's poor. Treat yourself to a little indulgence; otherwise you're no help to the people who need it most. Be a little bad!

If you don't help other women, you can go to hell—any of them.

Look out for your sisters; otherwise, save us a seat in the underworld!!

See? We've basically taught you everything you need to know about being a strong, flawless feminist woman. But before we leave you, you have to . . .

---

* Or guy! We love guys!!

** If you're not sure what kind of lumps you have or what we're talking about, please see a doctor.

SIGN THE CONTRACT

You're almost there! Almost. Before we give you our stamp of 100 percent fully feminist approval, you must sign the contract below:

This binding contract is made this _____ day of _____, 20___, by and between Reductress and _____("the Feminist"), in order to promote the goals of The Feminist Cause™. In order to accomplish the aforesaid, the parties desire to join together in a binding partnership under and pursuant to the Women Helping Women Partnership Act, amended from time to time ("the Act"). The Feminist is hereby required to not fuck this thing up, and in good faith will pursue The Feminist Cause™ to the best of her ability, even if she's tired or just doesn't want to deal.

NOW THEREFORE, the parties *her*to do *herby* promise, covenant, and agree as follows:

Section 1. Name

The signatory of this agreement agrees to go by the label "Feminist" from this day forth on all formal documents, Twitter bios, dating profiles, tattoos, interviews, talks with family over Thanksgiving, weddings, funerals, live births, and one-woman shows.

Section 2. Business and Purpose

The business and purposes of the Partnership are to uphold, manage, operate, and sell and/or yell the principles of feminism as needed.

Reductress may, at its discretion, request that the signatory purchase and distribute a yet-to-be-determined number of copies of *How to Win at Feminism* or share her copy with her broke friends in exchange for some hummus.

Section 3. Morals Clause

As a Feminist, the signatory is hereby subject to all the collective scrutiny of her fellow feminists, as follows:

   i. All of her words, tweets, and grams must be in accordance with all feminist standards.

  ii. Her appearance must represent the cause of feminism in a positive, empowering, and flawless light.

 iii. She must pursue her career with the intensity of a feminist.

  iv. Her sex life and partner(s) must reflect the values of feminism.

   v. She must be an active advocate for others while also making time for herself.

  vi. She must have a cool haircut that is feminine but still edgy and young but not scary.

 vii. She vows to love hummus forever.

_____

FEMINIST SIGNATURE

Please sign and mail your copy of this agreement to the Reductress offices in order to be considered an official member of The Feminist Cause™:

1 REDUCTRESS WAY
SOHO, NY 100100

Congrats! It's official! You are now a feminist. Now that you're part of the team, check out our . . .

Blooper Reel!

WRITING THIS BOOK WAS A BLAST! AND WE GOT UP TO SOME CRAZY HIJINKS IN THE PROCESS. LOL!!!

HERE'S US WRITING CHAPTER 1! AHAHAH, LOOK AT BETH'S FACE! SHE RUINED THE COMPUTER, AND LOST US EIGHT CHAPTERS OF THIS BOOK! LOLOL!!

WE GOT IDENTITY THEFTED!!! UGH OOPS LOL!!!

OOPS! WE CALLED OUR INTERN MEGAN FOR TWO MONTHS WHEN HER NAME IS ACTUALLY CARMEN!!! SORRY, CARMEN!!!

CONFERENCE CALL!!! LOL!!!

AT THE END OF THE DAY, WE'RE JUST A BUNCH OF CUTE KLUTZES WHO WROTE AN EFFING BOOK!!

ACKNOWLEDGMENTS

Wow! What a book. We honestly can't stop writing until we thank all of the people that helped make this beautiful chunk of 100% recycled paper happen.

First, we want to thank our amazing illustrators, Steve Dressler and Carly Monardo. We'd also like to thank our designers, Tom Pappalardo and Kris Tobiassen.

Hats off to our photographer who flew in all the way from Chicago, Kendall Burke.

Thank you to our amazing and brilliant editor, Hilary Lawson, who we were pretty sure we would drive insane by the end of this, but she seems to have not lost it yet. This book would not be here without Hilary being on board from start to finish. Somebody buy that girl a drink.

We also want to thank our hilarious and sometimes-brave models you see throughout this book: Alex Grace Paul, Alise Morales, April Lavalle, Colin Heasley, Courtney Wielgus, Doug Widick, Evan Barden, Hannah Murphy (who isn't afraid to take her top off in the middle of New York—it's perfectly legal!!), Janani Sreenivasan, Jasmine Pierce, Jewel Elizabeth, Jordan Mendoza, Julia Hynes, Lacey Jeka, Lucy Cottrell, Madonna Refugia (who also donated an actual photo from adolescence), Matt Little, Matt Rogers, Meagan Kensil, Mitra Jouhari, Nick Kanellis, Nicole Silverberg, and Skyler Bingham.

We want to thank all the feminists who are currently winning, sort of winning, or at least doing their best to win. You all get an "F" for "Feminism!"

Speaking of that, we want to thank feminism itself for existing; without it, this book never would have happened.

We want to thank Beyoncé, Lena Dunham, Sheryl Sandberg, Ruth Bader Ginsburg, Oprah, and a popular lotion-making company for providing us with so much inspiration.

INDEX

Page references followed by *p* indicate a photograph.